Hearts Immersed Within

By Renee Sellers Bennett

Renee Sellers Bennett

Copyright

DEDICATION

Marcenia Hope Vaughn Stone
Lee Anna Brown Sellers
Imogene Stone Jacquays
Gwendolyn Stone
Mary Helen Stone Andrews
Sue Stone Hooper
Winnie Virginia Garrett Bennett
Marie Bennett Stevenson
Mary Ella Miller Jones
Mary Frances Jones Bennett
Recoursah

and

To my precious family who have given me
their love and support.

In Memory of
Michelle and Anna

Disclaimer of Ignorance

In the South, we mean what we say, but we don't always say what we mean. A true Southerner will sometimes leave a few words out of a sentence, but more often than not, we add some extra words. The effort gets the job done, but other times, our words leave the listener scratching their heads. A Southerner may also exchange a word or words *every now and then* to *put* some emphasis on what they are *trying* to *say*. There, that was a perfect example of our lingo. The proper way to have made that statement might read, "A Southerner may frequently exchange a word or words to place emphasis on what they wish to convey." It is not that we are uneducated; it is a subconscious choice that we often make to add drama to our conversations. Don't forget, when we speak our propensity to make a one syllable word into two is our trademark.

Our words define who we are in the South, but please don't judge us too harshly when we ramble on or sometimes just forget to finish a sentence. For the most part, we are gracious, loving and kind. So please be kind as you read my written expression as I will sometimes ramble on and revert to the lingo that easily rolls from my tongue to the tips of my fingers. It is a prerequisite to Southern charm.

Inspiration

Who is Recoursah, pronounced Re – core – suh, and what part does she play in a story that intertwines the lives of the southern women that shaped my journey of love, laughter, and the joy of southern cooking? The following pages chronicle an ordinary life, nothing spectacular and spellbinding, but a compilation of experiences that I hope will warm your heart and engage your soul. You will learn who Recoursah was and what she represents in the heart of a southern girl.   But first, journey with me to a place and time when Sundays meant church and "Sunday Dinner" at Grandma's house.   It is a lost time, before the erosion of the American family, a time when extended family was a powerful influence in shaping the ideals and values of the next generation. It is a time that impressed my young mind so strongly, putting me on the pathway to cherish and honor southern traditions.   Share   in   my story and in the shaping of a southern cook, spiced with humor and recollections that give insight into why cooking is so personal for me and so many others.

You will see many "I's" throughout, however, this book is about the people that shaped my life and made me the person I am today. Without them, "I" would not exist. It's my interpretation of a simple life as I saw it then, and still continue to see it today - filled with southern women who influenced my ideals and me as a person. I have endeavored to present a visual of the beloved family and friends that are woven into my heart, one that is as precise and colorful as they reside in my mind. Alas, they are there, branded on my soul. In the words of Ralph Waldo Emerson, "The years tell us much that the days never knew," how powerful that one statement is -and how compelling to me; after having lived just over half a century, as both a southern woman and one of the generation of baby boomers.   Meet the women who are and were the heart and soul of my family. Through my recollections, may you discover a correlation to your own loved ones and their purpose in your life. Meet the women who have been my inspiration.

My roots run from the North Georgia foothills to the suburbs of Atlanta, Georgia, crossing through Gwinnett County and Walton County both as a resident and a descendant. My paternal grandmother was born and reared in Gwinnett and her ideas and values were from the Victorian era – literally. Perhaps that is why my love of Victorian customs and décor is clearly seen in my home and shared with friends and family. They are a reminder of my heritage and representative of my passion for keeping family values of gracious living. I have tried to instill the values of respect and compassion in my children as they were instilled in me.

Lee Anna Brown Sellers was born in 1892 in Gwinnett County, Georgia. Her father was the schoolmaster in the tiny community of Gloster. Her mother died when she was in her early twenties, leaving her to help rear her younger siblings. She married in her thirties – an old maid of that time. She settled in Walton County in the town of Loganville and became the mother of two children, both boys. Lee Anna raised her two boys as the wife of a railroad worker, who later became a well-known and respected Chief of Police of the town. I did not really get to know my paternal grandfather. He had "hardening of the arteries" and was institutionalized when I was only nine. He lived there for about three years before his death. My memories of him are very vague and mainly consist of the smell of the Bengay®, a mentholated cream that he rubbed on his chest in the winter and the taste of cream peppermints buried in his pockets.

My grandmother Lee Anna, known as "Grandma" to us was reported to be a wonderful cook. She was sixty two when I was born. If I obtained any direction in her kitchen, it was through osmosis. It was like the ghost of kitchens past by the time I was old enough to take any interest in her instruction. In her earlier days, she cooked all the southern dishes and canned food just as most women of her time. I can't remember any of the dishes she prepared. I just heard about them from my father. She was an "old grandmother".

Grandma even cooked for the prisoners being held at the city jail, much like the fictitious "Aunt Bea" on the series Mayberry R.F.D., supporting my grandfather's position as chief of police. Let me just say that he was much more than a police chief. He was partly responsible for the original water lines in the town, literally, as

2

he dug many of them. He read the water meters, repaired the leaks and took care of the city. He was a one man show. Currently, his portrait hangs in the lobby of City Hall.

My earliest memories of my Grandma flash through my mind. She was a robust woman of about 5 feet 9 inches and what one would call back then, "big boned". Bless her heart - she had feet that were about a size ten, complete with bunions and corns to boot. Her hair was white – beautifully so, but my childlike assessment of her hair never formulated the words that would bestow praise upon her. She opted not to indulge in the bluing that many of the ladies her age used. Yes, blue hair! It was quite the fashion.

Grandma always had a dip of snuff in her mouth and sometimes it dried around the outside of her lips. I was never inclined to hug her and I didn't kiss her very often. I loved her, but from a distance - you know the kind of love born of awe and admiration, because after all, she was my father's mother. She was sort of an icon in that town and to me, one whose affection was an elusive presence.

Lee Anna

The Porch

Grandma was commanding in a room or just on her front porch. That is where I remember her best, sitting on her front porch, facing Main Street. Right next door to her was the Methodist Church that we attended. She lived in what was once the Methodist parsonage. The porch was at least fifteen feet wide and one and half that width in length. It was made of sand and mortar, and one only had to take a few short steps from the walkway to arrive in the sanctuary of its berth. As you turned to look back at the street, you could see seasonal flowers flanked on your right and left, nestled in flower pots, but more often than not, used coffee cans. The containers held many colorful flowers, but my favorite being the petunias. They weren't the modern day wave petunias, just the good old fashioned ones, whose fragrance shouted *spring in progress*. They were a reminder that spring was in the air, and summer just around the corner. I would find myself leaving the premises on many occasions with one of those old coffee cans filled with the sacred flowers with great intent to see them thrive. I am sure they would have bowed their heads in dismay if they had known that they would eventually shrivel up and die.

The chairs were fashioned of green metal, the standard porch attire in the 60's. Grandma sat in a massive Victorian wicker rocker that reminded me of a throne. I can't remember ever sitting in it, as though it was hallowed ground and the encroachment of little children would be unthinkable. Many times, beside the rocker, a large wicker basket held an array of books. They would have been checked out from the book mobile.

The mobile library came to town every few weeks, bringing the joy of reading to the doors of those who loved and craved the words that would take them to faraway places. I remember climbing on board the bookmobile with her, in awe of the shelves of books. My grandmother would make her selections, filled with pages that would soon occupy her basket and later occupy her mind for hours. She must have read hundreds.

Grandma's home was filled with her own books. It was not until I was older that I would appreciate her collection. Their musty smell was a deterrent in my younger years. Many of the books

4

whose copyright was from the early twentieth century contained peculiar phrases that were no longer used. I loved books then, and still love the powerful feel of a book in my hand.

Six Ounces

I must have made the always anticipated trip from that front porch to Grandma's kitchen a thousand times. There would be the small, white refrigerator, gallantly waiting and whose door would open with a tug on the silver handled lever. It always revealed small sized bottled Cokes®, six ounces to be exact. That was and still is six ounces of the most satisfying refreshment known to man in my estimation. There is just nothing better than a small bottled coke. Even now, the replica bottles are not the same. Somehow those six ounces of the captured refreshing drink can never be replicated in the more modern bottles. I was never disappointed and more often than not, I would find a tin tray of parched peanuts to accompany the drink. My fingers would become the captor of the parched peanuts, painstakingly removing them from their shell, divesting them of their skin. After drinking a few swallows of the coke, I would place the peanuts into the top of the bottle, and then settle down into one of Grandma's porch chairs. I sipped the coke through the peanuts, allowing a few of the nuts to slip into my mouth, a mixture of soft and crunchy. I was sated, indulging in the joy of what I thought was an art; one I had observed from my daddy.

Tell, Tale - The Gang's All Here

As a widow, my grandmother spent her days visiting with friends on her porch or theirs, reading her beloved books and working crossword puzzles. Grandma broke her hip around the age of eighty two and spent about two months in a nursing home. In defiance, she declared that she would not read or work her crossword puzzles anymore. She returned home to finish her days of living in the contentment of her home.

When Grandma turned ninety, I organized a surprise reception to be held in the church social hall, the only place fitting for the occasion. Her mind had been compromised by a series of mini strokes. When she arrived, slowly creeping on her walker, she began to exclaim, "Hail! Hail!" When I heard those first two, "hails," I was mortified that she was cursing in the church as the blasphemous words fell around my ears like the sound of an impending crash! The content of her sentence surely sounded like an expletive. Furthermore, I cringed that she was in front of her family and friends, holding my breath for what was to follow, then, hearing the remainder of the statement, "the gangs' all here!" It took me a moment to digest the context of her sentence. I breathed a sigh of relief, for I knew that sometimes she could drop a curse word or two. That phrase will stay with me forever. It was only recently that I discovered the origin which was the title song from a movie from the very early 1900's. My grandmother was only a teenager then.

In church, Grandma was quite embarrassing. She loved to sing,

6

always off key, and always too loud. The words, "Draw me nearer, nearer precious Lord," and "I Am Thine O' Lord" still reverberate in my mind. She lived in the church parsonage almost until the day she died, spending only a few short months in a nursing home. She was ninety seven. In her honor and at my request, "I am Thine O Lord" was sung at her funeral.

Mimi

My maternal grandmother who we fondly called "Mimi" was a pillar of strength and was probably one of the most influential women, other than my mother, that inspired my love for cooking in my younger years. She was a godly woman and never let a day go by that she did not offer love for Him and His praises. Mimi's quiet strength was born of a lifelong struggle, but a continued passion to serve God and those she loved. She was a legend in our family and to her credit, raised her children with great love, faith, and family values that continue to live on.

Marcenia Hope Vaughn was born in 1904 in Cumming, Georgia, the foothills of the North Georgia Mountains. She met and married her husband in her early twenties. He was nine years her senior. Their courtship was short lived as she had a very strict father, who would not allow "suitors" to visit in the home.

I am reminded of the lyric of a country song, "You start walking my way, I'll start walking mine, and we'll meet in the middle, 'neath that old Georgia Pine." Except in this case, my grandparents met at the church, but decided to have the preacher marry them in the middle of the road, in fear of my great grandfather's protestations, and the double barreled shotgun he was known to carry. They literally had a "shot gun wedding". I am certain they wanted to be able to make a fast getaway if he arrived before the marriage was sealed.

In my younger days, I would tell my friends about my grandmother's wedding. Finding her plight romantic as I imagined her there with the man she loved, standing in defiance of her father, just like a fairytale. I used the term "shotgun wedding", later learning of the misused connotation. For those who are in the dark, it means the mother is expecting a child before marriage and her parents are none too happy. Sorry Mimi for beseeching your honor.

Mimi and my Grandfather Stone stayed busy farming for a living, and producing a large family. They lived on sixty acres of what was termed "bottom land" beside the Chattahoochee River in Forsyth County. Mimi gave birth to the first of her eight children in 1924, all of whom were born at home. The children were born in two year intervals - a set of twins preceded the baby child in the family. My grandfather named all of them, but the youngest one. I don't know the origin of all of the girl's names, but my mother was named after a character in a love story. Her name is Dorrie – just think of sorry and pronounce it "Dorry".

My grandfather must have had an affinity for the hills of Georgia. There are two North Georgia mountain towns that are nearby to Forsyth, County so he named the twins after them – Helen and Hiawassee. Actually, their names were given as Martha Hiawassee and Mary Helen, but called Hiawassee and Helen. Hiawassee will always be Hiawassee to her family, but Martha to her friends. Once I was telling a friend how far away all of my aunts lived from the Atlanta area and how difficult it was to get together for the holidays. Explaining the distance in hours of time, I said, "Hiawassee is seven hours away from Atlanta". She looked at me very peculiarly and said, "No, Hiawassee is only about two hours from Atlanta!" I then explained, "That is my aunt's name - Hiawassee." My friend was a redhead with the propensity to turn as red as her hair. Let's just say, her hair paled in comparison to her face.

As I said before, my grandfather named all of the children with the exception of the baby and that was because of his untimely death. My grandmother was pregnant with baby number eight. The ages of the other children were eleven, nine, seven, five, three and the set of twins were twenty one months old for a total of two boys and five girls. Thomas Arthur Stone was hit by a car as he walked home one evening in November. He was left on the side of the road, and the hit and run driver was never found. He was transported to the morgue. There, as they were preparing to take care of the dead, he moved a toe. He was returned home and I am sure in haste. His internal injuries led to his subsequent death. The family was unaware of just how seriously he had been hurt. Unfortunately, he was never transported to the hospital and lived only a few days after his return home from the morgue. He died on Thanksgiving Day. Grandfather Stone was gone, and tough times were on the horizon. Arthur Sue, named after my deceased grandfather, was born the following March and thankfully would be called "Sue".

It was 1935 and the depression was in full swing. My grandmother could no longer farm the land. She owed a four hundred dollar debt against the property to the bank. The bank took the land, and she took the cow, the only thing she had of value, other than her eight precious children. She moved to Atlanta to be close to family. Living in several rental homes over a period of years, she finally settled into the East Point area in the suburbs of Atlanta, eventually buying her own home. Meanwhile, the stories of life unfolded and were later told to me by my mother, stories of love and great family ties that warm my heart today.

Rich in God's Blessings

As soon as the children were old enough to work and make a contribution, they did so. My grandmother kept her faith and kept her family in the church, even holding "prayer meeting" at her home on Friday nights. My mother has told me tales of how food was never plentiful, but love was always there. As a treat, on Fridays, before prayer meeting, my grandmother bought hotdogs and marshmallows to host a wiener roast. They had a neighbor who worked in a potato chip factory and she would bring a fresh bag of chips home every Friday night for the occasion. It was a difficult time for the Stone family, but the camaraderie was there, and of course God was at the helm. My mother has always told me, "I did not have a father here on earth, but I have always had a heavenly father."

The Stone family all had steely blue or piercing green eyes that could be seen from across the room, and they all flashed with indignation if anyone crossed any one of them. They were both proud and protective of one another. They were not to be reckoned with in the neighborhood. The girls were beauties and the boys were great protectors of them, except when it was their turn to wreak havoc on the girls, but always in fun. Recently, my mother's brother found a poem that they had to learn and recite at school. He mailed her a copy. It was a special gift from her brother and endearing to me. It brings the fall of the year to life and paints a picture of the Stone family, poor in earthly possessions, but rich in God's blessings – nature in its most vibrant beauty - a gift to rich and poor alike.

October's Party

October gave a party
The leaves by hundreds came
The chestnuts, Oaks and Maples
And leaves of every name
The sunshine spread a carpet
And everything was grand,
Miss Weather led the dancing,
Professor Wind the band
The chestnuts came in yellow,
The Oaks in crimson dressed;
The lovely Misses Maple
In scarlet looked their best.
All balanced to their partners,
And gaily fluttered by;
The sight was like a rainbow
New fallen from the sky.

By George Cooper

The Aunts

I can't really imagine how life would have been without my "aunts," an extension of my mother. How lucky could anyone be to have five sisters as my mother did? Sisters – the word is quite sacred in my family. All of them, in their way, played a role in shaping my thoughts and opinions of others. I placed them all on a pedestal, much higher than any of them would have aspired to be placed. Of course, they never knew how much I admired each of them and realized how much I was watching. Not until later years, did I discover that they were all flawed in some way, just as each and every one is as a human being- just as I am. Carefully and without knowing, they helped to mold me and shape many of my thoughts. No, they were not perfect, but they were mine, much admired and always loved.

Imogene or "I'm – jean," as she was so fondly called, was the oldest of all of the Stone family children. She married when she was seventeen and ditched her given name, shortening it to Jean. She had one son and eventually divorced, always working very hard to support her family and succeed in her career. She had an agenda of her own and that was to be successful, and she did succeed.

Jean abhorred her nose. It had a slight crook and was a trademark of the Vaughn side of my family. When I look back now, it is no surprise to me that she got a nose job. She was driven to be all she could be and apparently, her nose got in the way. I will never forget when she showed her new look riding in her convertible, of course with the top down. She looked like a movie star, I thought as we rode down Main Street, her nose tilted in the air. Jean always had my admiration. She was one hundred percent class. She wore the right clothes and jewelry. Jean had the figure of a model. She had an exotic look that was the envy of many I'm sure.

While working for an investment firm in Atlanta, Jean, at age forty, met and married a man twenty years her senior. She was able to travel extensively, both here and abroad. She and her husband owned a home in the up-scale Boca Raton, Florida and had a lodge in Northern Canada, dividing their time between each. She became the ultimate hostess, entertaining friends and family constantly. I don't really know if she aspired to become a gourmet cook, but she achieved that status. She was in her glory!

Jean and her husband, Dutch, lived during the winter months on one of the canals in Boca Raton in an upscale neighborhood. Their home was a beautiful ranch that was made for entertaining. Somewhere in my middle teen years, after ten to twelve hours of being cooped up in a car like sardines, we arrived in Boca Raton late on a Friday evening. There were the four of us children and Mother and Daddy, of course. We pulled into that posh neighborhood in our big ninety eight Oldsmobile. I am certain that the driveway was just long enough to accommodate the long and sprawling sedan. We had landed in the lap of luxury and didn't know the extent of our good fortune.

The L-shaped home surrounded a swimming pool on two sides and was covered by screening that formed a dome over the pool. I had never seen anything like it in my lifetime of limited travel. Entertaining was simplified as carefree tables were set around the pool for guests to indulge in the creations that came from that well-oiled machine that Jean called a kitchen. When we first entered the home, the smell of a standing rib roast permeated the air and we were well on our way to one of the most satisfying meals that I can remember. Tired and hungry after the long drive, our appetites were ferocious and we were not to be denied. The roast was heavenly, as were the twice baked potatoes. There was a salad and tiny sour dough rolls, but the crowning glory was yet to come. My eyes had feasted on the dessert, when I entered the kitchen. It was the Perfect Chocolate Cake and was deemed as such on the cover of the *McCAll's* magazine that proclaimed the cake's title. We had lemonade and tea to drink. I still enjoy lemonade as my beverage, when I try to duplicate her meal. I say duplicate, because the bar was high and I still struggle to pull my chin to that level.

The subsequent meals were just as enjoyable and well planned, as our activities for the remainder of our stay. The spark was lit and the fire burned bright to emulate her gracious entertaining skills. Fine food and great service may be enjoyed in a restaurant, but the experience can never hold a candle to being entertained in the home. The sense of hospitality cannot be replicated as far as I am concerned.

On that trip to Boca Raton, Florida, I discovered that cooking could engulf so much more - the art of entertaining. Yes, my mother entertained, but it was on a different level that focused on juggling the needs of four kids. She more or less entertained on a daily basis - that is entertaining the idea of what to cook for the next meal.

From that day forward, Jean was my inspiration, her flair was undeniable. I aspired to be like her in every way. She was the catalyst for my desire to experiment in later years with less traditional southern food. Will I or can I ever achieve fame in the art of cooking? I am certainly not a chef, but I could readily adapt to that title.

Anyone can be the perfect hostess, even with the bare necessities. A table setting with flowers gathered from your garden or a simple beautiful green leaf from a tree placed in a vase, speaks volumes. Taking the time to show you care makes the difference when entertaining. My fame remains to be seen, but I hope my reputation is on the same level as Jean's. In her beautiful and gracious home, I found a burning desire to be the ultimate hostess.

I was always in awe of her when she came to visit us. I loved her very expensive diamonds and emeralds – green was my favorite color. She played the role of the perfect hostess for twenty years and sadly died of lung cancer at the young age of sixty. I wish that she could have known how much she played a part in my kitchen ventures and my passion to entertain. Fate never gives us a glimpse of what we will become and how the roles of others will help to shape and mold us. Jean, you left us too soon.

Imogene

I will always treasure the first recipe that I was given by Jean. I share it with reverence.

Jean's Twice Baked Potatoes

Preheat oven to 400 degrees.

6 medium baked potatoes
1 c. sour cream
½ c. butter/margarine
½ lb. cooked bacon, drained and chopped
2 c. sharp cheddar cheese, grated
Salt and pepper to taste

Wash and pierce potatoes with a fork in the center of the longest side of the potato, so that if you sliced the potato in half lengthwise, the fork imprint would be your guide. Do not grease as skins will need to be tough. Place on oven rack and cook for 1 ½ to 2 hours or until potatoes are soft. Remove from oven. Using paper toweling that has been folded to from a barrier from your hand; slice the hot potatoes lengthwise into two halves. Immediately scoop the pulp of the potato into a mixing bowl, preferably a standing mixer, leaving the shell intact and a thin layer of pulp lining it. Add the margarine. With a hand mixer, beat the potatoes, along with the margarine to a smooth consistency. Add the sour cream and beat again until the consistency is again smooth. Place the shells on a baking sheet and fill with the potato mixture. Sprinkle with grated cheese and then bacon bits. Place in oven and heat for 10 to 15 minutes, or until potatoes are hot through and through.

Gwen

Every one of the sisters was close friends to one another. My mother was exceptionally close to the sister who was born two years after her. Her name was Gwen. Mother and Gwen were inseparable, as two peas in a pod. Many times, both of them would start to say the exact thing when they spoke. At age fourteen and sixteen, they had their first job in an ice cream store to earn money to contribute to the family income. They lied, telling their employer that they were twins, because Gwen was not old enough to work. They thought they had pulled a fast one on their employer, but I feel certain it was not an oversight. The two worked after school until midnight, cleaning and mopping the store before they could go home. As an added bonus, they were given pimento cheese sandwiches as an after school snack, a welcome treat for the two of them. They could not afford to buy anything extra and food at home was never plentiful. After working for hours, they went home and did their homework, collapsing into bed when they were through, only to get up and start it over again. They learned a lesson at a young age, to be productive and make a contribution to their family.

Gwen was perhaps the most beautiful; at least she was in my mother's eyes. She had eyes of green and soot black hair. Her skin was olive and she was of medium height, with what my mother thought was the perfect shape. As the two got older, they continued to share each other's thoughts and became almost as one. My mother has often told me stories of Gwen and how she always had everything in perfect order. She would wash and iron her clothes to perfection on the weekend, preparing them for work the next week. The gloves that she wore were as white as snow, as recanted by my mother and she was much admired by the others for her perfection. My mother married at age twenty one, but their bond was ever stronger.

Even though the family struggled through ups and downs, nothing could prepare them for the tragedy that would come to their door. It was an August day and twenty six year old Gwen had noticed something unusual for a female. Then, young women did not go to the gynecologist for regular check-ups, but she knew that she

17

should go. She made the decision to go to the doctor alone, and learned that she had "female cancer" on a follow-up visit. There wasn't any terminology given for the exact kind of cancer she had and technology was limited. Not to alarm anyone in the family, she scheduled a trip to North Carolina to a cancer treatment center, hoping for a more encouraging prognosis. Sadly, there was nothing more than the treatments she had been prescribed, no cure. She went back home to her family and shared the sad news.

Within two months Gwen was hospitalized and was administered cobalt, the cancer treatment of choice in the late fifties. Soon, a stroke paralyzed her on the left side, as the treatments wreaked havoc on her body. My grandmother never left her side. After six long months in the hospital, Gwen was given a reprieve as she begged to go home in the spring. She was released to her family, and their care, the only place that she really wanted to be in her final days.

The Stone family had welcomed my father into their family and loved him like a brother. My daddy loved Gwen like a sister and my mother has given me some insight into the depth of that love. One day, Gwen had requested to go outside to enjoy the fresh air, as she was not able in her sickened state. Honoring her request, and with supernatural strength, my daddy picked her up in the chaise and took her outside, so she could join her family. I can just visualize that scene as my mother described it to me. I am sure that Gwen was only a shadow of her former self after having her body ravaged with cancer and the treatment that was just as debilitating. The adrenalin rush my daddy must have felt as he lifted her proved to provide strength beyond the ordinary, giving my mother a memory to last a lifetime.

I visualize Gwen in my mind, lying on that chaise, her black hair, with eyes as green as the sea, just wishing for what we all take for granted - a breath of fresh air. She must have inhaled the sweet smell of spring with reverence - my daddy, the hero, standing there proud, not knowing that he had made such an impact, not knowing that the tears in his eyes would forever be remembered. I am sure he looked to be ten feet tall to those who witnessed this act of adrenalin controlled strength. To me, he has always been ten feet tall.

Throughout her illness, Gwen never lost her sense of humor and looked for any opportunity to have a good laugh. The shortness of life was her destiny, but humor and laughter was not to be denied. The neighbors must have been on alert under the circumstances of Gwen's illness, and curious each time they saw activity at the home. Once when she was being transported by ambulance to the hospital, she told the ambulance attendant, "Pull the sheet over my head, so the neighbors will think I'm dead!" I can only imagine the reaction of those attendants as she gave her strange request; I'm sure a welcome relief to what would have been a somber task. Life to her was to be savored and she chose to enjoy it as long as she could. In her darkest hours, she found the light of joy in a little humor.

When Gwen died in June, I was just shy of my fifth birthday. By then, almost all of my grandmother's children were married. I was one of the five grandchildren, whose number later grew to fourteen. Gwen was brought home after the funeral home had prepared her and placed in the living room for visitation, as was the custom during that time. I remember looking at her in her casket in her angelic beauty, unaware of what I was witnessing. I thought she was asleep. I don't remember any tears. I am sure that all the family members were careful not to alarm the children. I do remember being left at home for the funeral services. I don't remember with whom. It is a memory that finds me climbing up into the old Mimosa tree on the front lawn and singing the song about the biblical Zacchaeus, who was "Looking for the Lord to see!" The innocence of a child - looking for the Lord who had just taken an angel home - speaking volumes to any observer – the Lord in his perfect wisdom had garnered the faith of a child.

Someone put a vase of gardenias in the kitchen window to catch the summer breeze, and it caught my mother's memory, the smell forever etched in her mind. She can no longer tolerate the sweet and pungent odor. How do you get over that pain? I still see it in my mother's eyes when she talks about her beloved sister. I still feel a loss of someone I never got to know. She is still on the pedestal I put her on so very long ago – the forever perfect "aunt" and a sacred sister.

The Twins

Growing up, the twins, Helen and Hiawassee, were two of my favorite aunts. Hiawassee, to the best of my memory always lived away. She never failed to remember my sister and me on special occasions. Easter and our birthdays were her favorite. She would send us beautiful dresses, both handmade and purchased.

It was always exciting when she came to visit from her home in North Carolina. She would sometimes come by late at night on the trip to East Point. I will never forget one night in particular that she and her family stopped to visit us. It was a Saturday and mother had cooked a chicken to have for lunch after church the next day. My mother, the ultimate hostess quickly offered to serve the travel weary family a chicken sandwich. I knew that it was for our lunch the next day, and I couldn't quite understand her offer. At that point in my life, neither did I understand southern hospitality. I intervened with my comment, "But mother, we were going to have that for tomorrow's lunch." I was quickly corrected and reminded to use my manners. I think I was around six or seven years old. That was one of my first lessons about being a gracious southern hostess. The story was recanted to me on more than one occasion, as a reminder that good manners are always appropriate and very much appreciated. I am still reminded today of that episode.

Helen remained single until I was ten years old. She still lived at home. We often visited my grandmother and I would find myself mesmerized as she dressed for her dates. I would observe her, watching intently as she put on her make-up. The picture is so vivid to me now. She would paint a beauty mark on her face, you know, the one like Liz Taylor. I think she has always fancied herself in the league with Liz – Helen was just that exciting to me. Before she would leave for her date, my question to her was, "When are you coming back?" I will never forget the answer that I would hear each and every time, "Some golden daybreak." I didn't know what that meant, but I imagined she was going on some great adventure and gold would be abundant. Helen recently went on her final date and I am sure to endless golden daybreaks, as she recently passed away. She left behind the wonderful memories of food that she prepared, recipes stored in her mind and forever locked away.

As a tribute to Helen and my brother Billy who enjoys cooking, I must share a recipe that he gave me a few years ago. It is a complete meal. This is especially delicious on a cold day. Helen nick named him "Buster" in his early years. The name did not stick, but he has always been a "Buster".

Buster's Chicken and Vegetables

4-6 Chicken Breasts, bone-in
1 large sweet onion, peeled, halved and then quartered
20-24 baby carrots, washed and peeled
12-16 small red potatoes, washed and halved
1 10 ½ oz. can chicken broth
1 can of French style green beans, drained (2 cans if serving 6)
1¼ c. water
1 tsp. black pepper
1 tsp. salt
2 tbl. butter
2 tbl. vegetable oil
3 sprigs fresh or ½ tsp. dried rosemary

In a Dutch oven, melt butter on medium heat, add oil. Place chicken in oven and brown, then remove from pot. Add the onions, potatoes and carrots to pan drippings. Sauté, stirring gently for about five minutes to disperse the vegetables and distribute drippings. Remove vegetables and set aside. Add the chicken broth and water to the drippings, to raise the sediment, gently scraping the bottom of the oven. Return the chicken and vegetables to the oven. Sprinkle with salt and black pepper.   Place rosemary on top of chicken and vegetables. Cook for 1 hour on the stovetop. Baste the chicken and vegetables often. 15 minutes prior to completion of baking, pour the drained green beans in one section of the Dutch oven. When cooking time has been completed, remove from oven. Using a slotted spoon, arrange chicken and vegetables on a serving platter.

*You may cook in a large oven proof casserole by placing the chicken and vegetables in the dish. Pour the liquid from the Dutch oven over the chicken and vegetables, adding the seasonings as instructed above. When adding the green beans, pour half of the beans each on opposite sides of the casserole dish, for an attractive offering to serve on a buffet. You may serve with a salad and bread, if desired.

Bunny

There is always a baby in every family, when there is more than one child and the Stone family held no exception. Conceived before the death of her father, Baby Sue or "Bunny" as she was so fondly called never knew her father. The "baby in the family" syndrome did not escape the Stone family when it came to Sue and the attention showered on her.

On her first day of school, Sue walked back home and my grandmother could not bear to make her go back. Instead, she was treated to a Coke® and cheese crackers. The sisters envied her special treatment, but secretly knew that they would have done the same. Ironically, she did not become spoiled. She had the sweetest temperament. She grew up to become the diplomat in the family.

Sue made her home with her husband and raised her three boys in Murfreesboro, Tennessee. She loved her boys desperately, but I know she missed having a daughter. She always made a big deal out of my sister and me.

As life would have it, I saw her very little over the years. Occasional phone conversations were all that we shared. It was not enough, but it was all that we had and I cherish her love and support. Of all of the aunts, I looked more like Sue. And because of that, I believe we had a special bond. I looked up to her as a second mother and took some comfort in knowing that someday, if my mother were gone, I would have her. It did not happen that way. She died of lung cancer at age sixty eight.

To some extent, I think all of us have these preconceived notions of how life will play out. However, the man upstairs has the ultimate plan. My notion was that since Sue was six years younger than my mother, she would be around longer. I sought solace in the idea that my pain would lessen and she would be my rock if and when I lost my mother.

Sue's legacy was anchored in her faith in God and her reputation as a wonderful southern cook in her community. I saw something deeper in her - the spirit of compassion and the ability to make others feel special. I am certain that attribute was witnessed by friends and family alike.

Sue was a favorite at the fertilizer business that she and her husband owned and worked. The customers adored her. I can attest to that love. There were over five hundred guests received at the funeral home.

I had not traveled to Murfreesboro very often as an adult, as I was busy raising a family and trying to make every moment count. No one in that town knew me as my presence had been rare. I had no idea how much the impact of my resemblance to Sue would make on those friends who attended her funeral. At the service, I walked down the aisle of the church and the looks I received were of pure astonishment - a younger version of their beloved Sue – to her father's honor – a girl named Arthur Sue, a fact I did not know until later in life. To me she was "Sue" or her nickname "Bunny".

Mother and Daddy

What can I say about my mother? For me, she is the most important member of the Stone family and dearest to me - my mother. Can I tell you that she was and still is one of the most beautiful women I have ever seen? The stories she has told and continues to share are part of the fabric that is woven into my soul. They are a part of me and have influenced who I am. Quite without my mother knowing it, she branded my soul with a deep affection of love, family and faith in a way that paved my destiny to aspire to be the epitome of a southern woman – gentle and gracious at all times. Of course, I will always fall short of that illustrious title, but I will never stop trying.

Cupcake

Mother, the fourth child born in the Stone family made her debut on a September day. The delivering physician took his payment in the form of a suckling pig. Growing up, she was always teased by her siblings as being "traded for a pig". It was not uncommon in those days to barter for goods and services.

One of the first jobs she had was working at the Federal Reserve Bank in Atlanta, Georgia. What fun she had there as a messenger! She would take messages back and forth from office to office within the building. She even had to carry money down the sidewalk on Marietta Street in downtown Atlanta with armed guards as her escorts, to deliver it to other locations. That scene would be unheard of now. Imagine the six o'clock news!

I know my mother was as pretty as a picture and had to be a favorite of her coworkers. Her nearly black hair and green eyes were a show stopper, to say the least. She was five feet four and weighed about ninety eight pounds. She has a great sense of humor and practiced a bit of mischief at every opportunity back then, a trait she had cultivated with her sister Gwen. Her nickname at work was "Cupcake".

As a practical joke, she gave one of the guards a laxative disguised as a chocolate bar, putting him in quite a predicament, since he could not leave his post at any given moment to go to the bathroom. I am not sure how that escapade played out, but I am sure that he has never forgotten her and became reluctant to taste any chocolate bar, especially one given to him by a green eyed "Cupcake".

Once, while employed by the Federal Reserve, the trolley lines workers went on strike in the city of Atlanta. It turned out to be quite an adventure for my mother. She was picked up by a limousine from her humble home and delivered to work, then at the end of the day, she was taken back home. This went on for several weeks. What a royal ride that must have been! And speaking of royal, the yearly Christmas party was held at the prestigious and elite Piedmont Driving Club in downtown Atlanta. A little "Cupcake" from the south side of Atlanta and the struggling side of life, found herself being treated like a queen. She had the respect and affection of her work family. Mother was soon to meet her prince charming at a pool hall of all places, some forty miles away.

At the Federal Reserve Bank my mother met and became a dear friend to the person who would introduce her to my daddy. She would spend the weekend with her in Loganville, which was about thirty miles east of Atlanta. It was on one of these occasions that she met my father. She, along with her friend and her date, drove to the next town, east of Loganville – Monroe. There she met my father – at the pool hall. They stopped outside the hall, which was located in the downtown area of Monroe. It was taboo for proper ladies to enter the hall, so they waited as her friend's date went into the pool hall to find daddy for an introduction to my mother.

I can just see my future father strolling out to the car carrying his pool stick, with his blond curls that stacked high on his head in soft waves; looking like the king of the billiards. She was so pretty and he so handsome; I am convinced he must have looked so intimidating. Daddy had that Paul Newman look with those beautiful blue eyes that were bent at the corners and there was mom, with her stunning good looks. The rest is history. They fell in love, married and settled in Loganville. "Cupcake" had found her man.

Bill and Dorrie

I would be remiss if I didn't tell you about my father, William Brown Sellers, fondly known to everyone as Bill or Billy, the "y" an endearment when added to his name. He loved to call himself "Sweet William". He was one of a kind and a legend of his time. Everyone in the area knew my dad. He was a basketball star and quite the athlete. He played basketball in high school and later for North Georgia College, transferring to the University of Georgia, where he was on the gymnastics team – parallel bars were his sport at the university. He enlisted in the army and was a veteran of World War II.

Daddy also boxed for sport while growing up. One of his friends would collect bets when he boxed, so sure that my father would win, and he usually found himself making some quick cash. My daddy played basketball in community leagues until he was just past forty years old, scoring forty points on his fortieth birthday! He hunted and fished and loved the outdoors. He was an avid sportsman. But, most important, he was a man who loved and cared for people. He was my daddy.

One of the best stories that I remember was the trick that daddy played on some of his friends. There was a watermelon patch in town and the owner was known for his great tasting watermelons. On the sly, daddy made plans with the owner for what he thought was some good old fashioned fun. He told his friends of a plan to steal some of the watermelons that very night, and several of them were game for some excitement and the reward of the fruit. The boys crept into the patch and just as they were devouring some of the juicy melons, a gunshot rang out. Suddenly, my father dropped to the ground, lying very still as his partners in crime swiftly made their departure, leaving the wounded behind, or so they thought. Their conscience was their guide as they soon found their way to the police station and ultimately, repenting their sins to my Grandfather, who was the police chief at the time. Daddy appeared, finding it hard to suppress his laugher, after giving them the scare of their life.

Granddaddy gave them all a tongue lashing, including my father, and demanded a fine from each of them, to be paid the following Saturday. He knew full well it would require a confession to their parents, because money was not easy to come by in those days and those fine young men would be in lack of funds. It was the thirties and the Great Depression had taken its toll on most families.

27

He had no intention of keeping the money, just the enjoyment of teaching the boys a lesson.

One of the boys was a preacher's son and was reluctant to admit the error of his ways. He dug himself into a deeper hole. He stole some of his father's chickens and sold them to pay the fine. When he attempted to make restitution the next Saturday, my grandfather returned the money, explaining that it was a lesson they all needed to learn. It was too late for the preacher's son and too late for the chickens. He had a lot more to confess to his father than just a crawl in the watermelon patch. In my estimation, the confession he had to offer his father was nothing to crow about either.

Wings

My daddy, who was never sick and had never been prescribed any medication, was taken from us by a brain aneurysm that burst, leaving behind a strong body, but with a mind that could not or would not ever engage the present. He was sixty eight. He lived an additional nine years, to the credit of my mother, spending only the last two years of his life in a nursing facility. He could recognize his family members and occasionally a friend. But the elusive present was his enemy. His last days were spent as he always lived, never uttering a complaint.

Daddy was always known for using some very descriptive words when he expressed himself, but more so after the illness. As my sister sat with him on one occasion, during his final days, he looked above her and made an observation that only his eyes could see. He stated, "Look at the span on those angel wings!" In that moment, he was finally living in the present and the future was his to see.

Wings will forever be a symbol of our Daddy. How much he loved the outdoors and even the birds that he often hunted! He was an avid fan of the Georgia Bulldogs. I don't think anyone could love the University of Georgia and his beloved Bulldogs any more than he did.

Later in years, when my daughter graduated from the University of Georgia, my heart was heavy, knowing that my father would not witness the climatic event of her graduation ceremony.

We planned a celebratory luncheon to honor her accomplishment. I had stayed up late the night before, finalizing the food for the event. Driving home from the grocery store, I was feeling so sad that Daddy would not be there with us. I turned the radio up and the song that had reached its popularity the year my father had passed away began to play, proclaiming what I knew in my heart, "I am looking down from above." My heart soared as I felt my father's presence, and again the next day on my porch, there was no doubt. We had just finished eating lunch, when a bird landed in a tree, just outside the screened porch. He began to chirp so loud that we could not carry on our conversations. I just looked at the bird and said, "Hello! Daddy, we know how thrilled you are too!" God had sent his messenger to let us know how proud my daddy was of his granddaughter - the message did not fall on deaf ears.

Two years later when my youngest son graduated, I was not surprised at his own story and I have recanted it many times. As he was leaving to attend his graduation ceremony at the University of Georgia, he was visited by a feathered friend. Just as he was getting into his car, the bird landed on the basketball goal positioned next to my driveway. The bird proceeded to chirp in orchestrated song, just for my son to hear. God speaks to us and sometimes only quietly nudges us, waiting for us to pay attention to his words. Then other times, he screams for our attention. He chooses his manner of communication and for us the bird was his instrument, singing and chirping accolades from above. How appropriate for the message to come from the rim of a basketball goal, reminiscent of the sport my daddy loved so much. Yes, I believe.

Sweet William

Atlanta Highway

This is where my life story begins.   We lived on the Atlanta Highway in Loganville, that wound its way thirty miles west to Atlanta and about that same number east to Athens.   We rented a house; two rooms to be exact that had a large kitchen that connected to another room.   The main hall which would be very large and obsolete by today's standards separated the two families that occupied the house.   That house is where we lived until I was five years old.   There were three of us children, then. I had an older brother, Billy, and a younger sister, Jan.

If there has ever been a question as to what a child can remember and how early in life, let me assure you, I know that I have memories that had to have occurred between the age of three and five years old. I can remember our first house so vividly now. The house was built around the twenties, painted white with a wide front porch. The yard was large in the back and held enough charm to stir any child's imagination, at least mine.   There were dog pens that contained my daddy's hunting dogs, Big Boy and Red Gal, along with other canines of which I cannot name.

Owning Fear

Conquering fear is not easy when you are a small child. I was not particularly fond of any dog, much less the ones held in our own pens. I found myself too many times, held captive on the top of our sliding board by a boxer dog, the pet of the next door neighbor. Later, I was chased by a neighbor's collie dog across a field of cotton, located on the street behind our home.   I still remember running through those rows of cotton, desperately trying to leave the dog behind.   He eventually stopped his pursuit, and I arrived home unscathed, but with a lifelong fear of our canine friends.

If fear of the tangible can make one tremble, a deeper more sinister internalized fear can make one shudder - via the imagination. There is one frightening episode that I will never forget and it still plagues me today. Imagine yourself being trapped.

We had old fashioned linoleum rugs in the house. They were

31

purchased on a roll and installed by rolling them out into the room, leaving a border of wood floor showing around the edge. The rugs were printed with a design and used to cover the bare floors, adding character to a room. As time passed, the linoleum would wear out. Literally, a hole would form in the rug. These rugs were customarily replaced as they became worn.

On this particular day, we had removed a rug from the house and it was rolled up in our backyard. There it lay, screaming for attention at two children playing. It looked like a tunnel to us, I suppose, rolled up like a cylinder and waiting to be explored. My brother and I decided to crawl through the "tunnel". He started through first, and I soon found myself right behind him. He decided to stop at the other end. Much to my dismay, I could not go forward and I could not go back. I was trapped. I remember screaming to my brother to move forward. I was traumatized at the helpless state in which I found myself. As a result, I have been claustrophobic all of my life. I will not ride an elevator to this day, unless I have no choice. Who knows how long I was trapped, maybe seconds, maybe minutes – maybe an eternity? Fear has a way of capturing its prey and capitalizing on its vulnerability. It comes in darkness, it shadows the daylight and in the heart of a child, it lingers and sometimes follows them through adulthood.

Embracing Trust

Those vivid memories of that first home, even though we left it by the time I was five years old are a source of comfort and inspiration. I felt loved, even when nightfall came and the two room abode became dark and less than friendly to me. At night, my mother's hand would secret its way through the spindles of the baby bed in which I slept until far older than a babe. Her hand would find its culprit – my tiny hand eagerly awaiting her secure touch – holding it until I went to sleep – or so she says.

It was my daddy that proved to be my real hero. For instinctively, I knew he was a man of strength, both loving and firm in his interaction with me and my brother and sister. I was somewhat afraid, yet in awe of him. He was stern, firm and loving.

My Hero

My daddy watched the Friday night fights. He would sit in a chair from the kitchen that housed our dinette set. The table had a grayish white Formica top with silver sparkles ingrained in it and the legs were of black metal. The chairs were constructed of the same metal, with cushions of pink vinyl, with those same silver sparkles mimicked throughout the covering. Daddy would sit right in front of the black and white television. I can remember it being dark in the one room in which our family both slept and watched television. I would slip out of bed, then perch under Daddy's chair, just because I could fit quite nicely, thinking I had pulled one over on him. As I peered through his legs into the black and white TV set, there were boxers on the screen, punching one another. It was quite boring and I was not one bit interested in watching the fights. I just remember feeling very special, that I was witnessing something for grownups only. The memory is so vivid, and I can only guess that the attraction I found being perched under my daddy's chair must have brought me some sense of satisfaction and security. Who really knows why a memory is made? Perhaps for me, it was the reassurance that my big and powerful daddy was just a touch away.

Trusting and Believing

Trust can also result in disillusionment. I was to learn that lesson very early on in my young life on the Atlanta Highway. On one of my birthdays, I received a doll from my mother and father. It was one of those dolls that was about eight inches tall, with hair that looked like it was spun from soft silk. I am convinced the color of her hair was dark, like mine, purchased that way to encourage a little girl's dreams of becoming a lady and to look as elegant as the doll. The arms and legs were moveable, with eyes that would flutter open, and then close. She was a beauty and I played with her that day in the back of my dad's yellow panel truck, with a friend from the neighborhood.

The old panel truck that sat in the back of the yard had been retired after it was no longer serviceable, but it served well as a playhouse haven. It was quite a mansion for two little girls with imagination. We must have played for hours. I accidentally left the

34

doll in the truck that day, and when I went back to get it the next morning, it was gone. No one knew the doll was there, but my friend. It was my first experience of disappointment in people. It was the first, but certainly would not be the last. My mother replaced the doll, but I could not displace the disappointment that my friend had caused in me. I recently bought a doll similar in type to the one that was stolen. I felt a sense of satisfaction - reclaiming something I lost a long time ago. Yet, I could never reclaim the loss of trust that I experienced on that day.

There is another kind of trust, the trust of a child of its mother. Apparently, I took that trust to the highest level. Unbeknownst to my mother, I took everything literally. My mother did not realize, until I told her in later years, how everything that she said was gospel to me. She was shocked that her admonitions were taken to heart. When she said, "Close your eyes and go to sleep or the Sand Man will come and put sand in your eyes," I was scared he was going to come in my window at that old house on Atlanta Highway. It was not until I was much older that my fear of a dark window left me, but sometimes the fear silently reappeared.

Mother did not readily speak of hell, but I knew the devil lived there. I got the idea that if you were not always good, you might just find yourself landing there sometime. I was afraid that the devil would come out of the ground and take me away with him. Or I thought he would come right out of a sewer drain, so I walked in the middle of the street to avoid going to hell.

Mother would also tell me that if I did not eat, I would dry up and blow away. I fancied myself floating in the sky, like ashes in the wind, floating high, soaring and making dips, but never falling to the ground. So, I ate.

Early on, I found myself wanting to be a pleaser. My mother and both grandmothers' constant instruction on manners and being a lady made an impact I am sure. I wanted and needed their affirmation. I wanted to be validated and I still do. Is a person born to be a perfectionist or is it learned behavior? I still don't have the answer to that question and does it matter?

Running through the house has always been exciting for children, knowing that it is off limits makes it more so. We were no different, and one day our playfulness turned into a serious accident. The old white house that was our sacred and trusted territory was also our indoor playground. My brother and I were playing chase in the house. There was a pair of French doors there, looming in the hallway - a barrier in my swift approach. I crashed through one closed French door with a mighty force for a five year old, sticking my arm out and literally pushing through the glass. My arm was cut quite severely as it went through the window glass. The gash barely missed the main artery on the inside of my right arm and I might not be here today if it had, as we lived about ten miles from the nearest doctor.

My mother and daddy rushed me to the doctor's office. I am sure the ten miles for them seemed more like a hundred. My mother's reassurances were probably as much for her as they were for me. Her promise of colorforms if I would stop crying was like a carrot dangling in front of a hungry rabbit. Colorforms were like magic paper dolls, whose clothing stuck to them. I desperately wanted them as gifts were reserved for special occasions only. I must have decided that bravery was not a price too high to pay. I needed some magic on that traumatic day, and the lure of magic paper dolls were my comfort. I did stop crying.

The doctor deadened my arm for the twenty two stitches that the wound required. I remember trying to be brave and the more the doctor bragged on my courage, the harder I tried to impress him by remaining very still and quiet. My mother left the room, unable to witness the stitching of my arm and a five year old was elevated to stardom as she became the perfect patient, basking in the medical staff's praises. Those color forms were my reward, but my celebrity status far exceeded their worth. The memory of that day is never far away as the scar is reminder enough of conquered fear and resolve.

For my mother those early days of learning to cook in that house on Atlanta Highway turned into years of perfecting a wide array of dishes. She was especially talented in baking cakes and pies and never used a recipe for the pies and many times varied the recipes that she used for the cakes. She was not shy in the kitchen and welcomed the challenge of a husband who hunted and fished on a regular basis. Many of her recipes are original and to her credit – delicious. I cannot say that my mother had a specific book that she used. She has always just cooked from memory, not measuring anything. It was the custom then and I followed suit, cooking from memory – the best recipes to be found.

It has been a challenge to take the dishes that mother and I both have prepared, putting them to words, somewhat like putting words to music. The following recipes are a favorite, some chosen from Mother's own creations and most importantly from her years of repeated success.

Dorrie's Pasta Salad

Mother created this pasta salad that serves eight. It is best if made and refrigerated overnight. It is a great dish to feed a crowd by doubling the recipe.

1 16.5 oz. boxes multi-color twist pasta
¾ bottle of Italian Dressing with Romano Cheese
5 oz. sharp cheddar cheese, cubed
1 small can of sliced black olives, drained
¾ cup mayonnaise
1 8 oz. container of feta cheese
2 pickling cucumbers, peeled and cubed
2 medium tomatoes, chopped into ½ inch cubes

Cook and drain pasta as directed on box. Transfer to a large mixing bowl. Pour dressing over the pasta while warm and stir gently to distribute. Add the next four ingredients, again stirring gently. Cover and refrigerate 2 to 3 hours or overnight. Add the cucumbers and tomatoes just before serving.

Dorrie's Rice Pudding

This recipe is a favorite that mother created to eliminate using milk and sugar, yet giving an extra smooth and creamy texture to her wonderful rice pudding. Memories of Mimi's rice pudding come back as I feel a comfort in each and every bite. I wait for mother to prepare it, because it is always better that way. Once in a while, I take the plunge. If I am cooking rice for a meal, I just double the recipe and bake the pudding after dinner. I can't wait for breakfast!

Preheat oven to 350 degrees.

1 c. of uncooked rice
1 can of Eagle Brand Sweetened Condensed Milk
2 eggs, well beaten
½ stick of margarine
1/3 c. half and half or heavy cream
¼ c. sugar
1 tsp. vanilla flavoring

Cook rice as directed on package. Transfer rice to a medium mixing bowl. Use a fork to fluff the rice. Stir in the condensed milk, melted margarine and vanilla flavoring until well blended. Add the eggs, stirring until well blended. Pour into a greased 9X9 casserole dish.

Bake at 350 degrees until lightly brown and firm in the middle. Cool for 15 to 20 minutes before serving. The pudding is great hot, cold or just warm. You may add a dollop of whipped cream and garnish with a mint leaf.

*Raisins may be added to the mixture, if desired.

Pecan Street

As I said before, my daddy was loved by the community, and boy did he love his community. I think he was claimed by several families as one of their own. One of those was a generous couple who gave him some land to build a home, right in town and adjoining their property. That is what we say in the south "in town" – meaning, within a few blocks of the main street stores. "Uncle Roy and Aunt Clydene" loved my daddy like a son. They did not have any children of their own. Daddy hunted and fished with Uncle Roy like a father and son, while growing up. We knew they were not our blood aunt and uncle, but their titles never changed.

While our home was being built we left Atlanta Highway to live in another rental house. By that time, I was heading for my sixth birthday. We moved into a house which was also considered "in town", that again, was shared with another family, somewhat like a duplex, with a great hall as the divide.

In the spring of that year, Hiawassee mailed Jan and me each a red checked dress for Easter. The dresses had laced trimmed collars and puffed sleeves and sashes that tied with a bow in the back. They had crinolines sewn in at the waist and required a slip to keep the crinolines from scratching. We had our picture taken as we did every Easter, Jan with her beautiful blond curly hair and I with my thin, fine hair cut short. If my hair had any length on it, to look decent, it required curling. The curls never lasted much longer than the time it took to roll it into pin curls, then securing them with crisscrossed hair pins. It was obvious from my hairstyle in a picture she snapped of me with her camera; my mother's patience had worn as thin as the hair on my head.

Sometimes, my mother folded a piece of brown paper sack over the end of my lock of hair, then rolled it up toward the top of my head, then twisted the ends of the paper together. When removed, the lock of hair would have a formed a tight curl that could be brushed into a nice set that looked as natural as the spring blooms that had peeked their heads from the cold winter ground. But like the last claim of winter on unsuspecting new growth, the curls would become as limp and droopy as the blooms.

Headstrong

The time was approaching and I would finally start school. Each spring it was the custom in our school system to allow the upcoming first graders the chance to visit school for a day. Our school did not offer kindergarten, so I was more than ready to begin first grade. My mother has always called me headstrong and I guess by age six, I was well on the road to independence.

The present first graders would stay home for a holiday, so that the upcoming first graders could occupy their seats and get a taste of what it would be like to attend school. It was a most exciting day and soon it came to a close. I allowed the opportunity to become a "first grader for a day," cloud my judgment in making a good decision. I decided that I would just walk home by myself. The school was only a few blocks away, and I didn't bother to wait for my mother or let her know my intentions. I must have found it exhilarating to proceed down the sidewalk to walk the three blocks to our current residence.

After passing the old rock gym, I found myself directly in front of Miss Valley's home. Valley was her first name and the salutation of "Miss" was and is used loosely in the South as a term of respect, almost as an endearment, one that I will use frequently in my recollections.

Boy was Miss Valley a colorful character, literally, for unlike my grandmother, she did wear the bluing in her hair - the kind that was achieved at the weekly visit to the "beauty parlor," and if I must say so – she showed it proudly. She was a retired school teacher who often worked as a substitute. In later years, she would threaten to tack my dress to bottom of the desk if I didn't turn around and stop talking. That would be a criminal act these days, but she and my grandmother were old friends, which made me fair game for her empty threats.

Next on my trip of sheer independent pleasure was my grandmother's home, where I am sure that I stopped for one of her treasured bottled cokes. I can't say that I lingered there as I was probably anxious to reach my destination and experience the satisfaction that independence had delivered. My grandmother must have been unaware of my new found independence, because she did not question my intent or alert my mother.

I am sure; I felt a smug satisfaction as I continued on my journey, passing a most familiar sight and another home to our family, the Methodist Church. The oak lined sidewalk in front of the church was as familiar to me as the church's incredibly beautiful stained glass windows that I was so in awe of each Sunday morning. The recessed encasement in the stone walls of the church held the stained glass panes that depicted scenes from the Bible and will be forever revered by me and others alike.

Byrd's store was just past the church and the last place I passed before I crossed Main Street to arrive at my house. I did just that. I slipped past the local bank, turned the corner and within a few yards, arrived home. I don't remember getting spanked, but I do remember the lecture, perhaps softened just a bit, from relief of my safety. The pleaser in me battled with my independent side and on that day, my independence won.

The Forbidden

Just down the street and around the corner, my daddy would take a short walk to one of the stores which were located close to our temporary home. He was a bad influence on all of us children. It was nothing for him to bring home a carton of bottled Cokes®, six to be exact, and a package of pin wheels for an after dinner treat. The pin wheels were made of a cracker base, topped with marshmallow filling, and then coated with chocolate. They looked like they were formed in a miniature Bundt pan. They tasted something like a s'more. It was fun to eat the marshmallow topping from the treat and save the cookie to eat last. How could something so insignificant create such a poignant memory? Perhaps it was the warm and secure feeling that children have when they witness their parents sometimes throw caution to the wind and allow their children the forbidden, knowing in all actuality, there would be no long term repercussions. Teeth will not rot overnight and the world would not come to an end. Yes, that must have been it.

We lived on Pecan Street for only a few months and in that house, we were told that a new baby was going to be born the next February.

41

C.S. Floyd

C. S. Floyd Road was named after "Old Doctor Floyd," I am told. Was he always old or did he live to a ripe old age? We finally had a home of our own on C.S. Floyd Road. It was located right beside the school – the only school in town, housing grades first through twelve. Can I just tell you that we did not need a swing set, even though we did own one. We had an entire playground compete with swing sets, slides and jungle gyms at our disposal. It was a paradise and our home was new and the room I shared with Jan was green. What more could a little girl ask? We moved in our home in the fall and I started school for the first time – two life changing events.

I remember well that first year of school. The first day, I found a new friend. Her name was Jenny. We had reading time, and both of us were seated Indian style on the floor. Each time I scooted over, she would scoot closer to me. I liked the idea of a new friend.

Prior to first grade, the only female friend I had was Charlotte. We had to be driven to visit, even though we did not live that far away from one another. Our fathers had played together as boys and had grown up together. She was an only child. I loved to visit her, because she had a bedroom she did not have to share. The room was blue and had a floral bedspread of lavender and blue to the best of my recollection. But the best part was that she had white furniture and a bed with a canopy. I could only dream of having one someday. I thought she was so rich. At that time, not knowing how rich I was to have both brothers and a sister.

Fostering Character

Choosing cowardice was not a conscious choice, but joining with my friend won the day. Jenny's and my friendship had grown. Once she invited me over to her house and her mother asked if Jan could come too. Jenny did not want to share our time with a little sister, so she and I locked the door to her bedroom leaving Jan outside. I remember feeling awful when she would knock and we would not let her in the room. It was a big mistake.

Jan found something to occupy her time, until we finally were asked to open the door by Jenny's mom. Imagine how I felt at the sight of Jan who resembled a clown. She had gotten into Jenny's mother's lipstick. She had it all over her mouth and had also broken the stick.

I was embarrassed and felt awful, yet the feelings of shame were overcome by the pain I felt for my little sister who was obviously devastated with her circumstance. I felt so guilty for leaving her outside the door, not insisting that we let her in the room. She was my sister and I had ignored her. It was one of my first memories of feeling overwhelmed with compassion and my own shame. Jan was on one side of that door, and I was on the other with only my cowardice between us. I had let her down to join my friend, who was also a little sister herself, one who was probably enjoying her own independence by having a playmate other than her older sister. Compassion had taken root in my heart that day and a lesson that I would not soon forget.

Fulfillment

February soon came in that first year of school and Valentine's Day was on the horizon. I was so excited about that day and I could not wait to put valentines in the special boxes we had all made at school with our names on them. The shoe boxes, decorated with red construction paper and white paper doilies had taken on a new identity. They were now the vessels for valentine cards, filled with declarations of friendship and fondness. The anticipation of opening the boxes to discover and read the verses was much awaited as well as the Valentine's party. The heart shaped tea cake cookies, decorated in reds and pinks would place a distant second in the contest for the excitement I felt on that particular Valentine's Day. However, that excitement would be totally obscure in the eyes of my fellow classmates.

February thirteenth, my new baby brother Scott came into the world. I was absent from school. When I returned on the fourteenth, I was more excited about my new baby brother Scott than the Valentine's Day celebration at hand. No one seemed to care about my news and my disappointment was deeply felt. Fulfillment, measured in expectations of other's actions, results in disappointment. As a little girl, I didn't understand that. Even now, I am not sure that big girls really do either.

The Bible Lady

Time marched on to second grade and the thrill of having Mrs. Stevens as a teacher. She was a member of the Methodist Church that we attended. At that time, we had an assembly once a month and "The Bible Lady" came to our school to tell us how we could earn rewards for reading the Bible. To earn a reward, students had to memorize verses and recite them to their teacher, until she returned the next month. On her next visit, "The Bible Lady" would then make a presentation to the students who had been successful in memorizing and reciting the verses. The first level of award was a bookmark and it was for learning the verse, John 3:16. The ultimate goal was to recite enough verses to win the most coveted prize – a Bible. I still have my Bible today and remember reciting the verses to Mrs. Stevens. I will always treasure those memories, the feeling of accomplishment and now I often reflect on the practice of praying that is no longer acceptable in public schools. It's just another chip away at the society that molded my life and the distant refrain of "My Country Tis of Thee" hums silently in my mind. We sang it every day at school, immediately following prayer and the Pledge of Allegiance.

The Trade

My palate for a variety of foods began to develop early. Sour kraut was a common dish served in our home. My grandmother made the kraut in a churn and we always had it served on Thanksgiving. That same year in second grade, Mrs. Stevens reported to my mother, my exchange in the lunchroom of cake with icing for another student's sour kraut. I am not sure what I was thinking. I probably could have kept my cake and ate it too - and the other student's sour kraut. In later years, Mrs. Stevens had the Methodist Youth Fellowship to visit her home after church. She served datenut bread from a can, topped with cream cheese and had lemonade to drink. I don't think the other teens liked that combination or found it to their taste. I remember feeling very special as if I had been allowed to enter into a world for the palate that only proper ladies would enjoy.

My confidence was taken to a whole new level. I was a lady. At an early age, I had begun to cultivate the desire to become one and equated that desire to enjoying the delicacies served at a ladies tea - the sour kraut would still be held in high esteem, but not in the realm of datenut bread from a can.

Cat-Eye Glasses

When it was time for third grade, I waited on pins and needles for the announcement of my teacher's name. There comes a time when our endurance must be tested and I had had three good years of three wonderful teachers. It was time for the test. There were only two teachers for each grade level and I had a fifty-fifty chance that Miss Ila Stephens would be my teacher. Could the pleaser in me win the day, for I would surely need that characteristic to take on the much feared Miss Ila? The luck of the draw- I lost.

My brother Billy had Miss Ila as a teacher the year before and the stories I had heard were not pretty. He had been paddled on more than one occasion. Back then, paddling was an appropriate punishment for what the teacher would deem inappropriate behavior, maybe just talking too much. I remember him laughing on one of those occasions, because he had on new jeans, and he said the paddling did not really hurt. I knew it would take courage to endure a school year of Miss Ila's instruction. The thought of her now, conjures up visions of the old maid. She was wiry of stature and wore the fashionable bluing in her hair. She also wore shirt waist dresses that were made like a blouse and a skirt, sewn together at the waist. The skirt was gathered and worn with a belt. She finished her look with a pair of pumps. Her face was partially hidden with what we described as, "cat-eye glasses". The frames were shaped with lenses that from the nose reached to form a point on the corner of each of the eyes. Back then, if you wanted to look really chic, your glasses might have tiny rhinestones on the corners where the legs joined the frames. I must say, to my recollection, there were no sign of those sparkles found on her glasses, not even a glimmer - no hint that a real person existed behind those rims. The color seemed to blend with her hair as if they grew right from her head. Her look was stern and extended right down to the mouth that never cracked a smile, and if so, it left the receiver somewhat confused and unsure how to respond. She was feared by all of us in her classroom.

I was terrified for her to call on me in class - that I might give a wrong answer. When I would go to bed at night, I would lie there and start thinking about the next day. Mother and Daddy left the light on in the bathroom every night and we kept our bedroom doors open. In the room I shared with Jan, I lay there, and questioned myself as to whether or not I had completed the correct page of my homework. So afraid that I might have misunderstood the assignment, I would get up and lie down on my stomach, using the stream of light from the bathroom to complete the assignment on the following page – just in case. I endured many nights of missing sleep, but I managed to make it through unscathed. Summer break could not have come soon enough.

Chocolate Biscuits

As they say, pride goeth before a fall and I was soon to learn that my pride would take a tumble. Just before fourth grade began, a new preacher was assigned to preach at the Methodist church, and he and his family were new to our community. Our house was only a block away from my grandmother's home and just around the corner from the church parsonage on Fair Street. The preacher's daughter was my age and I quickly made a new friend. There were lots of children in the neighborhood and we were all allowed to visit one another freely. It was on one of those summer days, that I made my first debut in the kitchen. I planned a tea party for the two of us and our mothers. It was my bright idea to make some biscuits for the tea and since I had watched my mother many times in the kitchen, it should have been a breeze.

I wanted to surprise my mother with my creation, so she bravely allowed me in the kitchen without her assistance, to prepare for the tea party. First things first. The only kitchen experience I had was from sheer observation and the verbal instructions my mother had given me. I had been taught to wash and scrub my hands, before starting to cook. After completing what would be the easiest part of my task, I carefully removed her wooden biscuit bowl from the drawer in the refrigerator.

I had watched my mother make a "well" in the flour stored in the bowl. A well is made by taking your bare hand and twisting a fist in the middle of the flour. I didn't measure the shortening; I am certain, as I took it from the can just as my mother always did, never measuring. I must have visualized the amount my mother used, as I placed it in the middle of the well. I "cut the flour into the shortening" with my hand, not knowing what I was doing, and then I added buttermilk, again with no measurement. I soon had dough to which I added cocoa and sugar. I rolled the tea biscuits out by hand, just like the play dough that I was accustomed to using when making my own "play biscuits". Voila', chocolate biscuits! I remember they tasted awful and I was quite embarrassed, because the pleaser in me had turned me into a perfectionist. My pride was hurt. That was my first venture in the kitchen, but there would be many more to come. From that point, I studiously watched my mother and grandmother and most importantly, I was allowed to participate.

Discretion Equals Power

Cultivating discretion equals power as I was soon to learn. I had an amazing teacher in fourth grade. Mrs. Bennett was a teacher that I loved and admired. She was actually Uncle Roy's sister. Her favorite saying to us in the classroom when we would guess at an answer was, "You are just surmising". I thought that was a pretty big word for "guessing".

Mrs. Bennett was also quite inquisitive about my family, as there were several family connections. Her mother had lived across the street from us on the Atlanta Highway. My mother had always taught me not to answer questions about our family to anyone. One day after a battery of questions about how everyone was doing in my family and my repeated answer of "I don't know," Mrs. Bennett said, "You don't know anything do you!" I felt a sense of power that I had been successful in the art of being discreet. Sharing information should be one's own discretion, and in this case it was my mother's.

A Dirty Crime

A dirty crime was committed and subsequent endeavors were perpetuated as a cover-up, all without a moment's regret, for shame had been spared. It was the habit of Mrs. Bennett to inspect our fingernails, when she took a notion to do so. Invariably, it was never to my advantage, since at that age, playing outside was second nature to us all, and of course playing in the dirt was very much a part of that endeavor. Thank goodness, I did not sit close to the front of the classroom! She would begin her investigation on one side of the room and go down the rows of desks, checking student's nails to see if they were clean. I wanted to be so perfect in her eyes. I knew I could not let her down - or, myself for that matter, because humiliation had no place in my pursuit of perfection. I only hoped and prayed that she would find others who had committed the crime of dirty nails to deter her dissention upon my desk.

Once her investigation started, I would sit there - trying to unobtrusively lodge any dirt from my nails of which always seemed to be my adversary. The particles would sometimes embed themselves so deep underneath, that they would not budge! A quick trip to the mouth, to bite and peel the nail would cause me to skip a breath, risking the chance that Mrs. Bennett's keen eyes would set their sights on my indiscretion. Biting the nails was considered a faux pas as well! Upon her approach, I would display my newly manicured fingernails, then, I would breathe a sigh of relief. Yes, I was thankful that my seat was not on the first row, confident that she had not discovered my act of expunging the dirt that then lay microscopic, somewhere beneath my desk. Sighing, I knew that I had escaped the shame of "dirt beneath my nails" and again, I had made my mother proud.

Little White Lie

Sometimes, not being completely honest can result in a windfall of luck and the justification self-serving at the least, for I was truly sick. In July, after fourth grade, I had my tonsils removed. The operation took place in Atlanta and after a few days in the hospital, we traveled to Mimi's house, since it was close in proximity.

Mimi knew that I needed nourishment to get better, as I struggled to eat. I will never forget that she told me she would pay me two dollars to drink a cup of "pea soup". Actually, it was the broth from the peas she had cooked. Without regret, I took the two dollars, never admitting my secret. I loved the peas and the soup too! It must have been equally as easy to drink the soup as it was to take the two dollars.

I still love the soup from peas, especially from the ones that has been made from fresh "pink eyes". Now it is a glorious day, when I can spoon that soup over crumbled cornbread, lightly dotting the concoction with a smattering of the peas. And if I were a southerner in the true sense of the word, I would top it off with chopped onion. I always look forward to the days when the peas are in season and feasting on their goodness.

Making No Sense of Cents

Using the sixth sense was one that was foreign to me, but I was soon to learn to listen to its whisper. As a fifth grader, I was about to experience a form of cruelty that has been around since the beginning of time - bullying. It came in the form of shame – mine, but this time I did not own it. It happened at a birthday party.

A schoolmate invited everyone in the classroom to her party. She was not a close friend, but all children love a party and I was happy to go. Soon after the gifts were opened, she made the announcement that her gift of eight quarters were missing. Everyone started saying that they did not take them. I can still see the smirk of that girl and her cousin as they continued on their vendetta to embarrass and humiliate me. My sixth sense or something in my heart, told me I had to declare my innocence. Opening my purse to prove that I did not have the quarters resulted in a shock. There they were – staring up at me, multiple faces of Thomas Jefferson seemed to mock me as I was frozen in horror.

I was embarrassed, ashamed and humiliated! I knew that I had not taken the quarters, but how would anyone at the party believe me? It did not matter that my closest friends did. I had been framed to perpetuate a cruel joke – for me no joke. How could I ever save my reputation? My close friends believed in my innocence, but it was still an embarrassment. I "cried my heart out," and never forgot. Disappointment in human nature had again struck a cord and trustworthiness is a commodity that I learned does not exist in everyone.

The Middle Years

It seemed that most all of my teachers had connections to the community and since our community was so small, it was a sure bet that, again, I would be in the classroom with a teacher who knew my family well. My sixth grade teacher was Mrs. Hanson, the daughter of Mrs. Valley Hodges – one in the same, lifelong friend of my grandmother. Mrs. Hanson was wonderful and has always been remembered as one of my favorite teachers. To her credit, my math skills were finely tuned and would become an asset in the kitchen as far as recipes are concerned. She taught math in a fun and wonderful way. It was a daily competition to calculate and provide answers to math problems, as fast as we could in her classroom. My nickname in class was "computer". I am sure that her connotation was not meant to compliment me in the definition as we know computers today. I just had a knack of computing the answer in my head rather quickly. I still do that and leave others struggling to pull out their calculators. When recipes are cut in half or reduced in size, I still rely on her math instructions. I never would have thought that simple math could create a disaster if miscalculated in a recipe. May I say that I have never made a mistake along the way? Yes, but that just doesn't compute.

Best Friends

Equipped with a sense of accomplishment, I would journey through the middle school years, those years when feelings are tender and boundaries are set in whom we can trust and lasting friendships are formed. Those years seem to define who we are and where we will go and the people who will remain a constant. I was about to find the constant friend that would remain so throughout my school years. It was in the sixth grade that I became friends with Lynn. I had finally found someone who would keep and treasure all of my secrets, because middle school children, especially girls have lots of them. Caught somewhere between childhood and adolescence, I discovered and understood what a best friend to someone meant. I had moved into those difficult years of adolescence and because of our age difference I did not want to reveal the many confidences with Jan that Lynn and I shared. After all, she was only a pre-teen, too young for mature information!

I embraced my new confidante. We spent days together, sometimes almost a week at a time during summer vacations. I would spend a few nights with her and then she would spend a few nights with me. She lived in the country and I lived in town. She loved the freedom of riding bikes to the store, just a few blocks away and the close proximity of neighbors. I loved the countryside.

At my home we walked to school and played on the school grounds. I enjoyed getting to ride the school bus home with her, when sometimes I was allowed to spend the night on a school night. It was fun to ride the bus, since I always walked to school. We had central heat at my house; she had heaters at hers. But we nestled down in the warmth of stacks of blankets and all was well in the warmth of having a best friend.

Back then, people shared a phone line with neighbors to reduce the cost of a private line. Lynn's family had a "party line" and I am sure, if the neighbors who shared the line listened in to our conversations, they had a lot of good laughs. A "party line" meant that more than one family shared a phone line, each having a special ring to indicate the call belonged to that specific family. If the other family was so inclined, they could pick up their receiver and listen in on a conversation. I remember being cautioned by Lynn to be careful

51

of what we said in our conversations. Of course, our conversations consisted of the observations and thoughts of impending adulthood, but plenty filled with humor.

Lynn was one of nine children and some were already married. Sunday was family day and all of her family came to eat lunch. The older adults ate first and the younger children had to wait. I can't imagine pulling that on my family today. They would be appalled. It was on one of those family occasions that I began to entertain. I soon found that the adults liked for me to imitate others and I enjoyed making them laugh. I liked the feeling. I had found my niche and my insecurity at being a skinny middle schooler was hidden, tucked away, but always there on the inside.

Lynn and I stuck together like glue. The country girl and the city girl were bonded. Keep in mind that the town had only one red light – what a city!

Big Okra Cake

When Lynn and I entered sixth grade, we then became old enough to go to MYF – Methodist Youth Fellowship. Even though Lynn was a Baptist, she went to MYF with me.   It was held on Sunday evenings. It was there that I forged lasting friendships and memories to last a lifetime. For two consecutive years, she and I chose to go to summer camp in the North Georgia Mountains, Camp Glisson. There were several offerings for camp in bunk houses, but we wanted to venture out in the wilderness. Our camp was called Pioneer Camp. It sounded like a real challenge and believe me it was quite an experience. We slept and cooked all of our food outside. We had to build a fire to prepare our meals and were responsible for obtaining the supplies from the community commissary at the campsite.

My cooking skills were about to be tested, as I had much improved after the chocolate biscuit fiasco. At that point, I had been allowed more and more responsibility in our kitchen at home under the watchful eye of my mother and my confidence had been building.

It was my belief then, since I had some experience in the kitchen, that I was much more proficient in cooking, compared to my fellow campers. My sense of accomplishment was about to be destroyed. A couple of others and I were assigned to prepare okra for frying.

After washing and cutting up the okra pods for about twenty people, I decided that it needed to be washed again – big mistake. Don't ever wash okra after it has been sliced. It was a big slimy mess much to my dismay and the remote chance that any batter would stick to it was slim to none. The oversized iron skillet that we used over the fire was filled with oil and heated. The cornmeal that we used to dredge the okra would not adhere to the okra pieces, but instead it created one big blob. We attempted to fry it anyway as it was part of our meal. Once the okra was dropped in the hot grease, it took a life of its own and became one big blob. So much for my big idea of washing the okra after it had been cut. I was certainly no okra connoisseur, even though I had purported myself to be just that to those innocent victims who had put their trust in my judgment. For certain, I was not able to salvage the okra into anything more than a big okra cake, much less salvage my pride!

Lions, Tigers and Goats – Oh My!

The local churches were the hub of any social activity in Loganville other than the occasional street dance that was periodically held. The street would be cordoned off by a flatbed truck for the musicians to play, and the pavement magically became the dance floor. The local movie theatre was also quite a drawing card, housing smoking rooms for those who wished to smoke as they watched the movies. The smoke was so thick; you could cut it with a knife. In those tiny rooms that held their victims captive, the smoke silently stole away the unknown.

Only in a small town suffering from the lack of cultural events could one experience the excitement that comes from the arrival of an icon. About once a year, the legendary "Goatman" came to visit, riding on a wagon, pulled by goats. He was usually granted permission by one of the local businesses to set up camp for a few days to peddle his wares and be the subject of the curious as they studied his strange appearance. His beard was long and gray and his clothing resembled the homeless of today. Furthermore, his homeless state by today's standards was rather evident as his wagon and encampment appeared to be all he owned, along with the flesh and blood of the goats that carried him from town to town. My memory of his visit will always leave a lasting impression and the memory of his stench likewise.

It was in the fall of my twelfth year that a new and entirely different attraction came to our town - the circus; never before had our town been the host to such a crowd drawing venue.

Living beside the school had its advantages. Imagine, having a huge playground at your disposal. The school grounds, which were literally just a step away from home, consisted of several open acres of land, just waiting for our exploration. On this occasion, the big top was planted right next door to us on school property. I can't imagine how that arrangement was constituted, even in those days.

I remember that there were lions, tigers and elephants. Yes, I said elephants. For some reason, the grass must have looked greener on our property, as we found an elephant in our own back yard, feasting on the long green grass, his caretaker oblivious to any wrong doing. Imagine my parents, when they discovered the beast snacking on the green. My mother was mortified and we were mesmerized – watching her from the window, as she communicated to the non-English speaking caretaker to remove the elephant. He got the message, as he was soon directing his charge back to the school property. We had a great story to tell at school the next day, but I am not sure we were believed, as even now, the story sounds a little dicey.

The Chosen Ones

We were the chosen ones – the few that lived in the school neighborhood and allowed to enter the sacred halls of the school long after the sounds of laugher had disappeared for the summer break. The one thing "the chosen ones" looked forward to the most was helping our teachers after all the other children had gone home for the summer. We were elevated to a status that made us the envy of many of our friends. Several of us in the neighborhood helped the teachers to put the books away in the "book room". We were also recruited to assist in distributing report cards to parents, but the monetary reward was a pittance compared to the sense of importance we all felt.

One of the most cherished items that is in my possession today is a beloved book that was given to me by seventh grade teacher, Mrs. Broadnax, cherished because it was a gift from her. The book is titled, "Readings in Georgia Literature," copy written in 1937. It has selections from some of the greatest Georgia Literature works in the eighteenth and nineteenth century.

A favorite selection is a poem that has been near to my heart. We formed clubs in the neighborhood and we always had a devotional. We patterned our clubs after ones from school and followed the protocol we had been taught. This poem is one I read at club meetings because inspirational messages were a part of that teaching. I will forever be grateful to Mrs. Brodnax for my gift. It has a special meaning to me, because I appreciate the beauty of poetry, some of its meaning so profound. The words of this poem are powerful and the title telling; the insight of the author holds forever truthful. Sticks and stones will break my bones, but words will never hurt me- poignant words close to a middle schooler's heart.

Words

God grant that I may,
With wisdom choose
The words I use;
That they may go
On winged note,
Enchanted words
From my throat;
Artistic words
From my pen,
Painting beauty
Now and then,
God let me ever see
Words are a gift,
From you to me
Fashioned of immortality!

by Clara Lundie Askew

The following recipe was given to me by Mrs. Broadnax. As I said, she was loved by all of her students and was a kind and gentle soul that all of us adored. This recipe was so simple for me to make when I was only twelve years old. It is so easy to put together in a hurry as a fabulous dessert that will garner you rave reviews. I keep nuts and commercial whipped topping on hand, stored in the freezer. You may serve with whipped topping or ice cream, or just by itself. It has a nutty macaroon taste and is so yummy.

Mock Pecan Pie

3 egg whites
1 c. sugar
1 tsp. baking powder
1 tsp. vanilla
16 Ritz® crackers (crumbled - not crushed)
1/2 to 1 cup of pecans (I use 1 cup)

Place the first 4 ingredients in a 2 quart mixing bowl. Beat until the consistency of a meringue, thick and fluffy, but not firm. Fold in pecans and crackers. Bake in a greased pie pan 30-35 minutes at 300 degrees until light brown. Serve with a dollop of whipped cream.

Apart from being The Chosen Ones, we were all also the neighbor of the school principal. He lived next door with one small exception, the school and its grounds were in the middle. So it was that I was technically living next door to his son, Jeff, who was the love of my life and had been since I was in the fourth grade. He did not share in the adoration that I had for him. I loved him from near and afar. Near, because he was my brother's good friend and we all played together on our big school playground. Afar, because I was so shy, I would never have let on how much I really liked him.

Eighth grade was my turning point. It was a chance to venture into unchartered territory. I was finally a teenager and eager to cross over the threshold of young adulthood. I was becoming braver and more confident, instead of the shy little girl, I had always been. My confidence was about to be shattered with the snip of scissors.

A pixie is described in the dictionary as a fairy or sprite, mischievous one. I was certainly small in stature at age thirteen, somewhat like a fairy and I guess a little mischievous. But, is that any reason for me to look the part? I would soon experience one of the worst days that I could have imagined. It was just before the beginning of the eighth grade. My mother took me to the beauty shop for a haircut and under her direction, the stylist began cutting my hair and it got shorter and shorter – the style evolved into what was termed then as a pixie! I was in full agreement as the stylist and my mother began their praises of how great it looked. Yes, a pixie. I looked like one of Santa's elves without his hat, when the dastardly deed was done. No going back. There was a feeling of unease as I realized that my look would be permanent, at least for many, many months to come and I had a feeling of dread when I looked in the mirror.

As fate would have it, Jeff was at our house when we returned home from the hairdresser. My mother offered to take him home and he climbed in the back seat. I was in the front seat, already nervous to be riding in the same car with him. Then my mother spoke the words that would soon haunt me each and every time I allowed my mind to revisit that fateful ride. "How do you like Renee's hair?" He quickly replied, "I don't like girls with short hair!" I was mortified and I imagined myself slowly becoming non-existent in that front seat, devoid of human matter – grateful the trip only lasted for the five minutes of eternity that it took to deliver him home. Take a dagger and put it through my heart, better yet, take a muzzle and put it on my mother for the next four years. It took half of my high school career for my hair to grow back. My hair grew very slow. I survived. Then the love of my life moved away and he became a distant memory as a new world of high school memories was made and childhood crushes faded away.

A Love Poem

A few months after the dreaded "pixie" haircut, I must have really hurt Jan's feelings, it appears very deeply. My mother kept a letter that Jan wrote to me which painfully shares the adoration of a younger sister to an older sister, who was in the throes of becoming a teenager – hormonal and a bundle of emotions. Pair that with the curse of the "late bloomer" and you have "Teenzilla". As I re-read the words recently and do the math, Jan and I were midway through our eleventh and fourteenth years, respectively. I try to imagine what I could have done that prompted this outpouring of pain and adoration.

The letter read:

A Love Poem
February 1, 1968

Trouble, Trouble, Trouble
That's all I ever make
If you had a sister as sweet and pretty as mine
And all you made was trouble
Wouldn't you feel like crying?

P.S. My sister is so sweet and pretty.

Wow! What a life lesson that is to read! During that time, I was feeling like I was the ugliest person on earth and there my sister thought I was pretty, and I was pretty to her. Even though my actions must have been ugly, she still held me in high esteem. I guess I really knew that back then. I just wish that I had not forgotten it on the day she wrote the letter – a pixie in need of some fairy dust made of kindness.

Summers on C. S. Floyd

As I said, being one of The Chosen Ones was partly due to the geographical location of those of us who were lucky enough to live in close proximity to the school. I am sure that our respect and admiration of our teachers was also part of the equation. Teachers were some of the most respected members of our town, along with the clergy. Our school years built character, integrity, courage and a sense of accomplishment. But, the summers were the most memorable days of my young life. They were the total sum of my existence and the feeling was mutual for my brothers and sister. I am sure the neighborhood children felt the same way too.

We could hardly wait for Bible School and all of the fun that we shared with friends as we embarked on those wonderful holidays called summer. It was a welcome reprieve from the long and tedious days of school, filled with singing, praising and lots of fun. We marched into the sanctuary to begin our day. We sang both religious and fun songs, one of my favorites being *The Grand Old Duke of York*. When he marched his thousand men up the hill, we stood up and then sat when he marched them down again. There was a morning devotional and we always said the Pledge of Allegiance. Crafts were made and stories of the Bible were taught to us daily. We walked to Bible school and then rushed home for lunch, which might include a picnic.

Our week culminated in an orchestrated program, and then our parents would visit our classrooms to see the crafts we had made. I remember the excitement I experienced as I looked forward to my parents seeing my artwork made of corn kernels glued to construction paper, depicting what we had learned that week.

The simplicity of it all, speaks volumes. Memories were created in the minds of impressionable children. We were not the children of technology. We were the children of the intangible world that exposed us to honor and values. We did not hold phones or computers in our hand. Instead we held innocence.

And then there were the long hot days of summer that followed our week of Bible School. Summer time meant blackberry jam, warm blackberry jam. My mother would pick the berries from the fence at the back of our property and make the jam for breakfast. She cooked biscuits every day. We rarely had toast, unless it was cinnamon toast on the weekends. Just imagine a hot buttered biscuit and warm jam every morning. It was a piece of heaven. She used those luscious berries in cobblers too. No need for ice cream to mask their wonderful flavor.

Days were filled with the fun and excitement of playing - days of wonderful memories that conjured up warm feelings of love of family, and for me, my special sister. Since my baby brother is seven years younger, he was like our child – a chance to practice motherhood. He survived somehow.

The Big Sister

The Yard: A Sanctuary of Affection

When my parents built our home on C. S. Floyd, they left the barn that Uncle Roy had built on the property. It was our sanctuary and had a personality of its own. A new wooden floor and steps that led to the loft had been added to the barn when the house was built. Old furniture was stored there and it was a paradise. The outside wood was dark and weathered. The roof was tin and small squares were cut into the wood in the eaves, the former home to Uncle Roy's beloved pigeons.

The barn had character and was as formidable as any castle in our eyes. It still had one of the old original doors. We swung on that door and rode it with all of our might standing on the cross pieces, holding on for dear life- sometimes pretending to be on a big black horse.

Our barn was hallowed ground and the haven for our playhouse, literally, since the entire inside was just that. The weather was never a deterrent for "playing house" for us. When it rained, it was even more exciting – it felt cozy. In fact, the barn was so large that we had more than one playhouse inside. Since, I was the oldest and in charge, I thought it was my right that I should have the best playhouse. It was downstairs. There I cooked with leaves for butterbeans and dirt for flour and invited Jan over for dinner.

We played everything from being pioneers, pilgrims, Indian squaws, mothers, daughters and orphans. As I got older, I liked the orphan scenario. I had to explain to Jan why we lived in our "apartment houses," without parents. She lived upstairs alone and I lived alone downstairs. Each and every time, I would begin our pretend session by telling Jan that our parents were dead and each and every time, she would start crying. I knew it would happen, but in my mind, we could not play without the scenario in place. I would comfort her and she would dry up her tears. The orphans were young adults. They had boyfriends, who were actually wooden posts and kissing was testy as splinters were a hazard to the lips - innocent lips.

Was the dialogue of having deceased parents necessary? In my estimation, the answer was yes. My perfectionism guided my imagination and ruled even when I would play.

Play we did, with gusto of unrivaled zeal. We played outside from sun-up until sun down and sometimes afterwards. We went from neighbor home to neighbor home and the neighborhood children did likewise. My mother took us on picnics in the nearby woods, just on the other side of the school. She would pack egg salad sandwiches, chips and cold Cokes® in the bottles. We would find a place on the "flat rocks" and spread our picnic out there. The rocks were very large and flat surfaced the ground. We lived in close proximity to Stone Mountain and they were common around the area. There were prickly pears around the rocks and one had to be careful when walking barefoot. The prickly pears were similar to a cactus and had sharp needles that were like a dagger if you stepped on one. All of us experienced that fate on more than one occasion.

We loved to go barefoot and that was more acceptable then. Stores and businesses did not require shoes. Prior to the summer days, in the early spring, the rite of passage involved taking off your shoes the moment that you could feel the warmth of the sunshine, but still feel the chill of the grass as it touched your feet for the first time in months. It was an exhilarating feeling, a liberation from the wool socks and leather shoes that confined your toes – toes that begged for freedom. I still remember the feel of that sand between my toes on the school playground; the sensation of touching and feeling ingrained in perfect unison. Those same toes pushed deep into the damp sand, and the entire foot was covered and packed with it; a gentle and slow removal and viola', an imaginary frog house. We played "doodle bug", in that same sand - an act of trying to make a bug come out of the ground by singing a song and digging into it with a stick. We were uninhibited in our child's play, innocent of the big world around us.

We rode our bikes through the neighborhood and down the streets around town, like we owned the world and for that precious window of time, we did. There was very little traffic, and it was not uncommon to balance ourselves on the bikes, arms apart as though we were about to take flight – no hands on the handle bars, dare devils we were, alive with the wind in our faces. We sped through the streets with not a care in the world.

Sometimes we walked barefoot down the street, risking an occasional unseen rock that caused us to hobble, until the pain subsided. On other occasions, we would step in a tar puddle. Yes, I mean puddle. The roads back then were made of gravel and tar and in the summertime, it got hot – hot enough to melt the tar in places. The tar would stick to your foot and had to be removed with a solvent. Our mothers were never happy to see us approaching with black sticky feet, magnets for dirt and grass.

Homemade ice cream was a perfect way to end a summer day or a special activity for Sunday afternoon. We always had vanilla, but when peaches were in season, they found their way into the long awaited treat. The custard was made and added to the churn and after the ice and salt were packed around the churn, we all took turns turning the crank. It seemed like great fun; until it was your turn to turn the crank, then suddenly it became a job. What a blessing when electric ice cream makers were invented! They have saved many elbows, but in retrospect negated the thrill of experiencing the creation of the best treat known to man.

Patience is a virtue and one that children have to work on to achieve. Once when we were making ice cream, after cranking for a considerable time, the lid was removed from the cylinder. Our anticipation was over and soon the creamy goodness would be ours for the tasting. To our dismay, we found that the dasher was missing – the tool that turned the custard into ice cream. All of that work, the custard was just custard. Disappointment had come and hopes were dashed as anticipation of that cool and creamy treat was thwarted and the cranking would have to begin again. You can't churn ice cream, if the dasher is missing. It was a lesson that I would not soon forget, like making a cake without a mixer. We were not to be denied, as the ice cream soon became ours; a well-deserved prize for our act of labor. When our bowls were filled, my mother passed around the saltines. It was the custom of my family to buy a pound box of saltines to serve with the tasty treat; you know the old sweet and salty routine.

The dogs always gathered to gaze up with hungry eyes to beg for a morsel of anything we would send their way. Back then, there were no leash laws, but our dogs knew their place. They did not wander too far, comfortable in their own territory.

I was not too fond of dogs, as I have professed; I had been chased by a few unfriendly ones in my earlier years. I didn't care too much for their smell, since ours stayed outside, and I would not touch them without washing my hands. I did feel sorry for them when they looked up at me with those eyes, yearning to be petted. My heart would get the best of me, sometimes I would pet them, but most often I used a stick to rub their back or head. It was the most compassionate effort I could muster as far as dogs were concerned.

The Spook House

There was a vacant house in the neighborhood that we had christened, "the spook house" early on in our younger years. It was directly across from Uncle Roy and Aunt Clydene and around the corner from our house on C. S. Floyd. It had been vacant for years and the wood had become a faded gray from years of disrepair. Complete with hanging vines, it stood there eerily as we walked past during the day. Once in a while, on a dare, one of us would muster up the nerve to walk onto the porch and look in the window, only staying long enough for our feet to touch the creaking wooden boards.

When nighttime fell, it was not unusual for us to be out at a neighborhood house after dark. That was the way of the world back then, for the most part safe and secure. The quickest route to our home was to walk right past the "Spook House". There it loomed in the darkness; it seemed to beckon us to venture on the very soil that held its foundation. As we crept past the house, our hearts were in our throats as we felt our chests constrict.

I would try not to look that way and pretend I was somewhere else on my journey home. How many times did one of our dogs wander up on that porch, just out of our unsuspecting eye, to tread across the wooden porch slats and our very hearts, as the unmerciful fear gripped us like a vise? Fear, it sent us running for our lives and jumping over the hedges into the forbidden "Park", a parcel of land that was the property of and affectionately so named by Aunt Clydene. Our fear more than surpassed the retribution we would face, if she knew that we had treaded on sacred soil. We could only hope that our tracks would disappear and that the noise of our descent would be muffled by the snoring of the two who dwelled within the white clapboard house adjoining the park. Just a quick sprint across the next yard would take us to safety and calm to a thunderous heart.

The "Park" had been christened with that name by Aunt Clydene as far as I ever knew and if Uncle Roy had any claims to that sacred piece of property, it was to maintain its beauty. The parcel of land was on about a fourth of an acre, surrounded by enormous hedges that blocked the view of the passer by on both C. S. Floyd and Fair Streets. Inside, it was a paradise, filled with several very unusual trees and many flowers.

There was a fish pond on the end closest to the residence of Aunt Clydene and Uncle Roy. It was made of rock and the circumference was no larger than about fifteen feet. In the center was a bird bath that was elevated above the pool of water below, to serve as a refuge for the birds as they dove in and merrily splashed about. The edge of the pond was surrounded by beautiful flowers and greenery. The fish were Koi and were a source of fascination to us children, as we seized on any opportunity to admire them. Those opportunities only came when we found Uncle Roy cleaning around the pond. On more than one occasion, we slipped into the forbidden territory knowing full well that Aunt Clydene would not be happy. The grass was sacred in that private sanctuary of hers and if allowed, would be worn down if we made it our pathway.

Aunt Clydene was very prim and proper and not unlike my feared third grade teacher Miss Ila. She had some of the same characteristics and was also a teacher, although not in our school. I still remember her scolding us, for walking through the "Park," but not feeling too sympathetic to her pleas. Of course, we complied, but on the sly, it was a thrill to defy her without her knowledge. We were guilty, but innocent in our ignorance of the sanctity of the revered soil.

Teetering on the Fence

Just as my childhood was beginning to fade into warm and wonderful memories, so were the feelings of mixed emotions of passing over that threshold. It was exciting and confusing to say the least to approach the teen years. I was excited to be a teenager, pivoting back and forth between wanting to be all grown up and clinging to childhood and the neighborhood fun.

I guess that I wanted one last shot at childhood imagination. It was behind our house that I found a new interest. It was the old shed on the vacant land behind Uncle Roy and Aunt Clydene's house. I asked Uncle Roy if Jan and I could use it as a clubhouse and he agreed. We actually had to walk around the circumference of the fencing that separated our property to get to the shed.

It was to be a secret clubhouse and we wanted to be very selective of who was allowed to join the club. In fact, we wanted it to be so secret that even our parents could not know that we played there. We routinely slipped into the shed on the sly, hoping that we would be undetected. That was the summer that Jan cut her leg.

One particular day, we decided to climb over the fence that surrounded the clubhouse, instead of using the fence opening. The top of the fence had been strung with a couple of lines of barbed wire. I made it over, and Jan did too, but not without having two deep gashes cut into the back of her upper leg. I was terrified, not because I was worried about Jan's leg, but I did not want our mother to know our secret. I took Jan into the house and washed her wounds with soapy water, applied some alcohol and band aids and told her not to tell. She never did and I lived in fear that she would have "lock jaw," in other words known as tetanus. That wire was rusty.

The days turned into the "dog days of summer" when our vacation was winding down into finality and the relentless hot August would be upon us. My mother would say that the shadows were getting longer, which meant the days seemed to shorten as darkness began earlier and earlier. But we welcomed the impending fall, school would begin again and our days would turn into a new routine. We would soon put away our short sleeved shirts and shorts. Our bare feet would once again be pushed into the confines of shoes and the sound of the familiar school bell would signal the time to meet our teachers, old friends and the challenge of gaining new knowledge. But we were equipped anew with the memories of summer and the sounds of laughter were never far from our minds, the camaraderie of siblings and neighborhood friends lingered well after the ringing of the morning bell.

Autumn

Halloween was always an exciting time of the year. The smells of fall were fresh in our minds as the long lazy days of summer would be a distant memory. The crisp air signaled the holidays that would follow, but first we would celebrate at our school with a carnival. Before the carnival began, chicken and dressing with all of the trimmings were served at our school cafeteria in the evening, and parents were invited. For a minimal fee, mothers could enjoy a welcome respite from the kitchen.

Then, the old rock gym would open for the festivities. There was a booth set up so that we could "go fishing" for prizes that was among some of the games offered. The cake walk was always in full operation, with a chance to win one of the coveted cakes that were made and donated from the parents of the school children. Each cake was numbered and placed on a platform. Participants paid to walk around the display of cakes to the sound of music. When the music stopped, if you were standing on the number drawn that matched the cake number, you won a cake. It was somewhat like musical chairs, but with a much sweeter prize. The carnival also had a "spook house" located underneath the bleachers in the gym, which was the dressing room for the basketball players. It did not have windows and was ideal for giving us a scare.

All of the school children would dress in costumes that were either purchased or created to attend the carnival. I, along with my brothers and sister chose the more creative route, and likewise became creative in fashioning our own "spook house" at home. Since we felt like we had a real one in our neighborhood, we were fascinated with the idea of creating our own.

We charged a quarter to our friends and neighbors to go through the "spook house" we had created, which was located under our house in the crawlspace. The mummy that moved its arms wildly was controlled from the air vent by strings that were fed through the cracks. Just the smell of the red clay under the house alone was a reminder to the visitor that they were in un-chartered territory, at least by those brave enough to indulge. It was good clean fun.

69

In later years, the appeal of our "spook house" was still there, but a step toward puberty transformed our thoughts and the barn. It became the site of a wonderful Halloween party; after all, it was hallowed ground. The plan began as an idea to have our own Halloween party with a few neighborhood friends, to include a trip to the spook house. It evolved into the entire seventh grade being invited and suddenly the impromptu party turned into a large gathering. The class only numbered fifty students. Of course, everyone did not come and I am sure that the number was less than twenty, but I can remember my daddy's excitement as the numbers grew. He made his late night trip to the grocery store to bring us all bottled Coke® and cookies. I am not sure that he could afford to treat us all, but he did not hesitate in his duty as host.

We played records and danced that first year. I can remember a girl that twisted the night away and I trying out the dance called the "Monkey," feeling very grown up. As an encore, the next years' event was just as memorable. "Spin the Bottle" was the highlight of the evening, but a trip around the barn with my secret love was not in the cards for me. I had never been kissed and my imagination had been peaked by both television and my friends recanting their own experience. It would be a long time before I would experience that sensation. Then it did not matter, that old barn had been transformed from a play house into a dance hall where young women and young men alike danced on the threshold of innocence and flirted with the road to adulthood.

As we grew older, Jan became a little more precocious than I, and I found myself defending her in the neighborhood and holding my mother at bay when she got into a little trouble. Once, she and a neighborhood girl decided to throw pears from another neighbor's yard into the middle of Main Street. I was so totally embarrassed when the local police made the girls clean up the mess.

It was not until later on in our lives that I found out that Jan would slip out of the house with a neighborhood girl and be a dare devil. She would climb out the window as I slept, clueless to her mission. Sometimes, she would take her pillow and then escape to the flagpole in front of the school, slipping it into the roping that daily sent the American flag to its final destination atop the pole. She would then take turns with her friend sitting in the cradle that the pillow had made, each spinning the other around in circles, defying retribution for their act. They never got caught and later I was a little envious of her defiance, as I never had the nerve to do such.

Christmas on C. S. Floyd

Do children today experience the amazement and wonder that Christmas day brought to the children of my generation? Can their feelings equal what I remember on that sacred and magical day? I pray so. Christmas was unadulterated magic to me and a precious time of memories never to be forgotten. Atlanta Highway memories are really fuzzy, just a Christmas tree of cedar with big light bulbs, the thrill of tossing the tinsel icicles for decoration is the highlight of my memory, and of course a new doll.

C. S. Floyd Christmas was met with great anticipation. It would mean trips to downtown Atlanta to visit Santa and best of all, ride the Pink Pig. It was an annual journey for me and my brothers and sister. The Pink Pig was a rail car of sorts that sported the face of a pig and was painted pink. The body of the pig had caged doors that were lifted up to house the riders. I remember climbing in to the body of the pig with a mixture of fear and excitement, my claustrophobia holding me a prisoner, even on such an anticipated ride. I was paralyzed with the thought of being in a cage, but thrilled with the thought of looking down on pure magic. The pig was hoisted inside of *Rich's Department Store* high above the stores' many departments. The goal was to carry the youngsters who occupied its berth on a trip around the store, as they visually embraced the enchantment of Christmas as it dazzled below.

The Pink Pig still exists today, even though *Rich's Department Store* has long since closed its doors. The pig has been reborn in an outside setting at a shopping mall. The magic can never be equaled, at least not to a boomer from the 50's, whose heart was suspended in splendor far above the enchantment below.

Back on C. S. Floyd, Christmas meant pulling the big plastic Santa face out of the barn. The face was about two feet tall, sporting the customary red hat and rosy red cheeks. His presence in the window would soon signify the wonderment of the days to come and the anticipation of a Christmas tree to follow. He looked as jolly as could be with his big fat cheeks, so rosy red and a smile that was contagious when looked upon by the children that had long awaited his placement in the window. The grand finale, yet to come, would find us rushing outside to peer in the window at his arrival. He came alive as the one single bulb found inside the plastic face would light up, as my mother plugged him in for yet another year. Our hearts would be bursting with excitement, knowing that the "real" Santa would soon be making his way to C.S. Floyd. My skin still tingles as I am engulfed in the remembrance of the plastic Santa face, his expression unchangeable. I bought one at a thrift store a few years ago and now his lighted face shines down on my rendition of a candy shop that I assemble each Christmas in my home, and my skin tingles once again.

Visiting Kelly's department store was just as every day as going to the grocery store except during the Christmas season. Then, a portion of it was transformed into a toy store. It housed shining bicycles, dolls, tea sets, train tracks and much, much more.

Each and every Christmas, the elementary school classes took a field trip during the school day to Kelly's. The short walk from the school was only a few blocks away and for me a source of empowerment, because as far as I was concerned, that was my sidewalk, part of my territory. It was the same sidewalk that took me past my Grandma's house and the church I loved. We walked from the school campus with our teacher in the lead, paired with a partner, most often holding hands, an army of children. Our destination would find us wide eyed with wonderment and dreams of what Santa would bring. Mrs. Kelly would be there and under her supervision made sure that we only admired the toys that we craved to hold, keeping them new and unused for those children who were lucky enough to receive them. We dared not touch or spoil the toys under the watchful eye of Mrs. Kelly, but I savored the smell of the new doll that I would choose carefully and dream about nightly.

In our family, we were so happy for each and every thing that Santa had to bring. The gifts were scarce, but plentiful in our eyes. A doll, a tea set and always a new pair of pajamas were staples of Christmas morning. Even the year when I begged for a pony and a cowgirl suit, to the point of dreaming every night for them, I was still willing to accept my doll and tea set with a grateful heart. The pony ran away, or so I was told. The cowgirl suit was a distant memory as I touched the face of my new doll. The smell of the new rubber doll was like a healing balm to any disappointment that I might have felt. We were so innocent of the ways of the world, lost in the magic that only Christmas can bring.

As we got older, it became harder to close our eyes and wait for Christmas morning and the surprises it would bring. We became what we thought was very cunning in our sneaky mission to the Christmas tree and all of the treasures it would hold on Christmas morning. Our mission was made long before the break of dawn and it was a test of skills.

As I said before, our parents kept their bedroom door open at night. We would lie there on Christmas Eve, trying desperately to fall asleep, even if for just a few minutes, hoping our parents would do the same. Most of the time, we were unsuccessful, making the wait for us, long and arduous.

Finally when we thought our parents were fast asleep, we would slip to the door and slither like a snake down the crooked hall toward our destination. On more than one occasion, daddy's deep voice would break our concentration on the task ahead and we would become paralyzed! My father's voice was more than enough of a deterrent to continue on our journey. It was back to the bed to wait another eternity. But, if we got lucky, we would make it all the way down the hallway and then we were home free.

Looking at Christmas presents in the dark was plenty exciting as we had the added pleasure of touching them, etching in our minds the very feel of them, trying to make out just what the morning held in store. The trip back to the bedroom was just as tedious, as we did not want to wake our parents, hardly able to contain our excitement. Our new pajamas, our accomplices, made the journey more pleasurable as we snaked our way back to safety and the exhilaration of being undetected. As we grew older and knew in our hearts that the real Santa was in the room that held our parents, our conscience kept us from making that middle of the night excursion. Insightfully, we knew that we were robbing them of witnessing our pleasure when we saw what Santa had brought. We did not miss the gleam in their eyes as we showed them our bounty on Christmas morning – call it a child's intuition - call it maturity.

The true meaning of Christmas was not lost on those holiday traditions. We made our yearly pilgrimage to the Methodist Church to either participate in a musical play or just be a spectator to the wonderful gift of Christ, our Savior. He was paramount in our focus during the season, because we were taught as much. The magic of Santa Claus would soon be fleeting, along with childhood innocence, but the mystery of the story of Christ would sustain us.

Going Home

C.S. Floyd Road is only a few miles away from where I live today. It looks rather foreign to me as I drive down the road that will shortly take me to my childhood home. When I make that turn in to the driveway that was the stage for a fourth of July parade and the launching pad for a first bike ride, I am home.

There are those of us who cannot go home, will not go or it is just physically impossible. I treasure the opportunity and if I am lucky enough to go when school is in session, I can only close my eyes, as the sound of children playing at recess takes me quickly down the path to childhood.

When I hear their shrieks of laughter, I become one of them, breathing in the smells of the glorious outside air, cold or warm, filling my lungs, giving me a dose of vitality. I imagine running across the playground, headed for the swing that will carry me far and above the ground, and as I fly seamlessly, the wind whispers making me as one of the winged creatures that I have always admired. I jump from the swing, defying gravity to land on two feet, reflections of an acrobat. The sliding board calls my name and I race to the steps, gingerly taking them two at a time, until I am at the top. Grasping the handles by the hand, I launch myself, becoming a missile, sailing at a breakneck speed until I reach the soft sand with my toes. The excitement is contagious and I see the other children following suit.

Next is the jungle gym, I climb to the top and hang by my toes. *Oh my goodness, if one of my children had ever done that, I would have had a heart attack!* My energy spent, I find myself beneath the enormous pecan tree, still standing strong. I drop to the soft and damp sand beneath the tree, placing my bare foot in a mound of particles, completely covering it. I firmly pack it around my foot then slowly remove it to make yet another "frog house".

Suddenly, I open my eyes and I am back to reality, my childhood slipping away once again; the sounds of children playing music still in my ears. I was one of them once and forever branded of the pure exhilaration of just being a child – innocent of the challenges and rewards of life to come.

I was only sixteen when I wrote the following poem and my perspective of life - the challenging teen years with their ups and downs, I am sure weighing heavy on my mind - the challenge of becoming a young lady. I did not share my poetry very often, finding myself an awkward little girl with dreams bigger than myself – ideas of what and how life should be embraced.

Shattered Dreams

Mary had a little lamb,
One and one makes two.
Candles on a birthday cake,
Blow them out,
A wish comes true.
Does he love me?
Does he not?
Oh tell me daisy do
Oh to be a child again
Oaks from acorns grew
One and one make two
I believed it all, didn't you?

Farris Avenue

It is without measure the wealth of knowledge that I gleaned from my grandmother, Mimi. She was the epitome of strength, quietly so, with a calming presence of one who had been in charge for a long time. The peaceful little neighborhood in East Point on Farris Avenue was her home for over sixty years and the home of many memories for me and my family. The rectangular plot of land as small as a postage stamp, with a tiny front yard, and a back yard that doubled its size was the anchor of a frame house made of wood and siding.

In the front yard, there was a large oak tree, which I am told was the sanctuary for those who sought anonymity and refuge in its branches - even as young adults, my mom and her sister, hiding from unwanted suitors. The wide cement walkway ended after a trek of about ten yards to a set of two simple steps, painted a blue-gray, which met a screen door that merrily opened and closed hundreds of times for the children and grandchildren who seemed to enjoy the sound of the slamming door. The wooden porch floor was also painted the same blue-gray; its coziness welcomed us in its embrace.

The front door was stained light maple in color with three small window panes that formed a diagonal pattern on its upper section. The door swung open to a wide hallway that was about ten feet wide and fifteen feet long. The floor furnace was a source of great delight on cold winter days, but ominous in its presence of the danger of getting burned. We were warned repeatedly to be careful, and somehow survived without any serious accidents.

There was a standalone cedar closet behind the front door that housed linens and across the hallway, on the left, nestled in between two doorways, a buffet. Beside the buffet was a phone chair that held a square black phone, that rung with frequency. Both of the rooms off the hallway had been bedrooms for eight children and a mother at one time, but eventually became a combination of living and bedroom space. At the end of the hall was the one and only bathroom. It was small, but adequate, housing a claw foot tub. To the right of the hallway was a door that led to a large room that held a dining area and day bed.

The remaining room was the kitchen. The kitchen – heart and soul of the house was small, but efficient. My cooking journey truly began in the house that had been home to a mother and the children who occupied four rooms and a bath. It was there that I was given the freedom to experiment and experience the pleasure of cooking.

Jan and I spent many summer days with Mimi, sometimes a week at a time. During the day, we helped her to can and freeze. I don't really recall exactly how many of those summer trips we made over the years to Mimi's home, but certainly know the moments were priceless.

We learned to peel and dice potatoes for homemade vegetable soup and shelled peas and beans. There were times that our only job was to keep the dishes washed as we worked to put away fresh summer vegetables for cold winter days.

Let me first say that I was the receptive student, eager to drink in all of the techniques Mimi had to share. I absorbed her instruction like a sponge and my "pleaser" personality made it more the easier. Jan was younger and not nearly as interested.

Mimi had apple trees in her back yard, and I found myself climbing up the trees to shake the limbs or to pick a few to send them on their way to becoming apple jelly. Some found their way to drying screens, fashioned from screen doors. Those were the best, because they were used to make fried apple pies.

Yes, Mimi did it all then and we were her willing helpers. It was our summer camp. We learned to cook and clean. We learned to take pride and reverence in the kitchen. But our lessons did not remain there; instead they spilled over to a space with a heart beating just as fervently as the one in the kitchen itself. It was the front porch.

In the evenings, if we were through with our work, the front porch would be our destination to rest. Sometimes, it was just an extension of our work space and we would continue in our endeavors - shelling peas or snapping beans. And if so, the rhythm of our work was made easy as the wisdom of Mimi's words taught us life lessons.

The long and narrow porch was screened. Loropetalum bushes grew outside in front and provided a feeling of being in a lush paradise. The red and white metal rocking chairs beckoned us to sit a while. The chair backs and seats were designed with small square holes for ventilation, creating cooler seating on those summer nights. It was Mimi's front porch, her haven and ours for those precious hours of time we spent sequestered there, the screens the only barrier between us and the world outside.

At the end of the porch was the seating I remember best - a matching red and white glider. It would carry Jan and me on many rides as we would send it creaking back and forth, sometimes building the speed so fast that it would threaten to come off the hinges, or so we thought.

The three of us would sit there on the porch - sometimes until the morning hours. There were times, the heat was so stifling, with hardly a breeze on those hot and sultry Georgia evenings, but we welcomed our time on the porch. Mimi would tell us stories of my mother and her brothers and sisters, as we took pleasure in imagining them as children our age, relating to them as more than just a mother, aunts or uncles. I remember them as champions of one another and defenders of the world outside.

I most recently added a screen porch to my home. And now my long last friend has finally come home, along with the memories of Mimi and the hours we spent on her front porch. The old red and white glider is missing, but I am creating my own memories. It beckons friends and family to stay awhile to revel in the pleasure of "porch sitting" and the pleasure of its refuge.

Pink Pleasure

In the one and only bathroom at the end of Mimi's hallway there is a memory carved in pink. It is a most beautiful sight after it had been extracted from its wrapper and laid lovingly on a big fluffy white towel beside a claw foot tub. The scent is subtle, yet soothing. It is a pink bar of Dove® soap, humble in its appearance, yet its significance speaks volumes.

There are a few things in life that are unequivocally afforded only by the rich. Then there are some things that the rich probably could never really appreciate. One of those things is a simple bar of soap. You could argue that point, as I am sure there are bars of which the rich pay a pretty penny, for soap that is.

As our world has turned to more and more luxury items for

the not so rich and famous, body wash has become the "new" soap. Not to say that the old fashioned soaps do not occupy merchant's shelves, claiming their fair share of space and surely sales, which brings me to the subject at hand; a bar of *Dove®* soap, pink to be exact.

Nothing can be more relaxing and invigorating than a nice warm bath. At the end of the day, Mimi had the insight in perfect perspective. She knew that we could not resist the opportunity to indulge in the warm and relaxing water in her claw foot tub. However, the pink *Dove®* bar was Mimi's secret weapon. We rubbed it vigorously against our skin to create poofs of enchantment. The poofs of suds composed of bubbles dissipated as quickly as they were formed. They rose and fell on our skin as they melted into sweet deliciousness. Mimi knew we would stay in the water until our fingers resembled a prune and the chill bumps on our bodies would rival the size of a marble. It was her tranquilizer of sorts, a way to coerce Jan and I to relax as we would soon make our way to our final destination for the evening, the back room.

The Back Room

As sure as the sun does shine, so did the time come that we had to go to bed, of course under the cover of darkness. I remember Mimi's bedroom so well, referred to us as the "back room". It had twelve foot ceilings and walls of plaster. The walls were painted a slate blue. There were two double beds, both had white chenille bedspreads, one was made of iron and the other a hard rock maple.

The two windows were high off the ground and Mimi kept the windows open to bring in the cooler night air, as there wasn't an air conditioner. Before we went to bed, we would comb her hair and spin it into a bun. She called it her "top knot". The three of us would climb into one of the double beds. Somehow the darkness, which seemed subdued on her front porch, became a looming presence.

I am certain that I took the middle spot on the bed, even though the big sister pretended to be brave, she was really very scared. I can remember just touching my Mimi with a toe, with the reassurance that her presence would get me through the night. The railroad was near and invariably the lonesome sound of a train would permeate the air. I recall the shiver that went up and down my spine as I lay there trying to be brave. It was a reminder that I was far away from home and no matter how much I loved my Mimi, I missed my family.

Then it would come. The whimpering would start, turning into a full and soulful cry. Mimi and I knew that it would come, just sure as we knew that the sun would again shine in the morning. After turning on the bathroom light and finally calming Jan down, we slept as well as anyone could between the heat and the tiny space allowed on the double bed. Sleeping apart from our Mimi was not an option, even though another bed was waiting for anyone who would be willing to turn back the "covers"- now that's a southernism.

The next day would bring loads of fun as we sat at the dresser in that "back room" and put on "our make-up" with Mimi's limited amount of face cream and powder. We would use her "bobby pins" to style our hair and pretend her slips were our dresses, using her gloves to give us the sophisticated look that we desired. Her good hats were off limits, but sometimes there was a chance to sneak an everyday hat on our heads. I don't once remember her chastising us for using her cream or powder. I just remember having fun pretending to be a lady. A few of her hats, now sit forlornly on my closet shelf, sometimes gingerly scrutinized and examined, as I imagine them on Mimi's head, and wonder what criteria she had in choosing them - if hats could talk.

Enrichment on a Dime

It was not all work and no play when we would visit. We left the boundaries of Farris Avenue to learn and explore. Mimi did not drive, but we walked to the bus stop or the shopping center nearby. We rode the bus to downtown Atlanta and shopped at Macy's and Rich's. We went to the State Capital Building and there we visited the museum. My grandmother did not have any extra money to spend, but she always made sure that we had fun and she took us

82

places that were educational and affordable, most of those were free.

My favorite store was located in the shopping center that was within walking distance to where Mimi lived. She did not have a car and never learned to drive, which was not unusual then. We would walk to the "five and dime". It was on one of those trips that we were allowed to choose new underwear. There weren't any panties printed with storybook characters as our little girls have to choose from today.

My visual is very clear. The panties were made of nylon and had insets just above the leg, with a small accordion design. The colors were pink, blue and white. Yet, there was another choice. I chose red. I don't really know why. Maybe it was because I would become a Loganville Red Devil and play basketball in the revered rock gym which had been my daddy's own turf. Maybe it was because I would grow to love the Georgia Bulldogs and their red and black colors and pledge my allegiance to them someday. Maybe it was the thrill of independence from conformity in its simplest form; daring to be unique. I wonder.

It was in that same five and dime that I got lost, while on a visit with my mother. It was not a very big store, but when you are a little girl it was quite large. After searching for what must have seemed like an eternity, I found myself crying for help, literally. When I was asked to describe my mother to my savior, it was later reported to me that I said, "She has black hair and red lips!" I remember those beautiful red lips and even then I knew she was a beauty, she was so pretty and I was so proud to call her my mother. She is still beautiful today.

Diversion to Wonderment

There were other diversions from those long summer days of cooking and preserving food. A trip to our cousin's house was a delight, especially since there was one girl. She was the only female cousin that Jan and I had. It did not matter that she was six years my junior, she was a female! Mimi's grandchildren numbered fourteen and only three of those were girls. Her father, my Uncle Tom lived only a few miles from my grandmother, and he would come to pick us up to spend time with his family.

I remember how excited I was to explore Uncle Tom's wonderful house that had an attic apartment. The home was quite beautiful, made of stone with a screened porch that was wide and inviting. There were window seats that housed storage space and a child's curiosity to peek inside was inevitable. Doorways were arched and even then my keen eye recognized the uniqueness of the home. It was a Sears and Roebuck house – the original cost was $750.00! The supplies were ordered from Sears and Roebuck along with the plans to build it. I can only imagine the cost to build that same home today with its exceptionality.

I had no qualms about visiting my uncle and aunt's home when my mother was not present, for I knew I was safe - safe from the dreaded torture of having a permanent wave set in my fine thin hair. When mother got tired of trying to roll my hair, only to see the curls fall out thirty minutes after the set was combed, her last resort was to ask for my Aunt Dot's help. That help meant the dreaded perm or a short haircut.

My aunt Dot was a "beautician" and had a beauty shop in the house. She was always more than willing to oblige my mother's wishes and submerge me in the shampoo bowl of no return. There were times that my fate had already been sealed even though my mother was not present. Aunt Dot would announce that she had been directed by my mother to put a perm in my hair. There would not be any running and hiding from her. I was not that daring and too ashamed to allow her to think I was not obedient. I could only try those kind of escapades when mother was present, convinced that she would change her mind, if I was out of sight. I remind my mother now of her brand of torture and of the results of the permanent wave that were not very appealing, as my school pictures can attest.

On one particular trip to my aunt and uncle's home, we were treated to the drive-in theatre. We all climbed into my uncle's station wagon. There were five of us children, along with my aunt and uncle. Our bounty included a large brown grocery bag full of popcorn that had been popped on the stove and much to my disappointment, chocolate covered raisins. What were my aunt and uncle thinking? What happened to the chocolate covered peanuts I usually ate at the movies? Where were the chocolate pin wheel cookies and Cokes® my daddy frequently brought home? Were my aunt and uncle from another planet? Surely my cousins had not suffered such an injustice at the hands of their parents each time they went to the drive-in?

I soon forgot the snacks as I was immediately engrossed by the big screen. Most of the limited movies I had seen were fairytales from *Disney*. Now, the screen held the images of the most amazing movie I had ever seen. The movie, *The Bible*, was bigger than life. I was mesmerized and fully engaged in the rare gift that would forever be remembered by a child who witnessed the parting of the waters and God's wonderment in full color. In that station wagon cramped with children, and an overdose of popcorn and chocolate covered raisins, the images of God's greatness was seared in my mind forever.

Sunday Dinner on Fair

When I was growing up, the term "dinner" was applicable to the meal that was eaten for our Sunday lunch. The term "dinner" was used loosely and often by many churches, almost fondly, as to encompass large amounts of great southern food. Supper was indicative of the evening meal. Dinner just meant so much more, food that is.

Every Sunday in my single years, we found ourselves on the long ride from Loganville to East Point, and the final destination - Fair Street. We looked forward to the wonderful meal that would have been prepared for us before we arrived. The trip was long and as always my stomach threatened my composure, forcing me to close my eyes and try to sleep away the "car sick feeling" that I could not squelch until we reached our destination. I would dash from the car and head for the kitchen, breathing in the smells and looking for a morsel to appease the sick feeling in my stomach.

Many times I would find warm rice pudding waiting for me to dive in for a bite. There could be stewed prunes left over from breakfast, still warm with a bit of margarine clinging to them. What child of this generation would eat prunes, much less stewed and seasoned with margarine? I would eat the sweet taste of the fruit, savoring each and every bite. Today prune cake is one of my favorites.

Mimi's meals were not always bountiful, but by today's standards, they were a feast. Fried chicken was usually the meat that was served, always accompanied with a few vegetables. Many times she added a small amount of corn meal to the breading on the chicken. Not since those days have I eaten fried chicken breaded in that manner.

The chicken was always a whole one that Mimi had cut up to fry. The sanctity of cutting up your own chicken has not been well preserved. Most people purchase ones that have been carved, fileted or de-boned into whatever fashion the butcher sees fit, thereby losing the most important piece of chicken, in my estimation – "the pulley bone." Yes, that's right. "Pulley bones," better known as "the wish bone" are now a thing of the past, along with the art of cutting it from both sides of the breast to form a most delicious piece of white meat for consumption; more importantly, the loss of the traditional breaking of the bone is just a memory.

Once the meat had been divested and cheerfully consumed, the highlight of the children's Sunday meal was for the lucky owner of the "pulley bone" to choose someone to help break it. The idea was that two people would grasp the prongs of the bone, one person for each prong, and then each would make a wish, then pulling on the bone, it would snap. The winner was the one with the largest piece and their wish would come true. ***Wishes, like magic were elusive and intangible, but we held them tight and smothered our hearts with their hope.***

My father loved the gizzard and would usually eat it before the meal was served. In the South, some of the fast food chicken restaurants serve gizzards and livers. I don't think I have ever heard of anyone serving a chicken heart. Not to let anything go to waste – Mimi fried the heart also. All of the children would fight over it. Can you imagine? There was only one heart, so it was first come, first served. I don't think any of my own children have ever eaten a chicken liver, much less a heart. They seem to be stable and not ill affected from the loss.

Once, after Sunday dinner, within weeks of Christmas, I slipped into the "back room" at Mimi's house. On this day, the "back room" housed a baby bed. That is where I hid. Boy was I sneaky. My mother and Mimi had gone into the "back room" to have a private conversation about Christmas. My name was the topic of conversation and I was glad that I was well hidden, as I sure that I was to be enlightened of a secret that had me trembling with anticipation.

My mother began to describe a most unusual gift that she had planned to give to me. It was a fur - lined pot, otherwise called a potty. The idea was that when I got up in the middle of the night to use it, the potty would be warm to my bottom. The two of them left the room and left me with visions of what the potty would look like. I spent hours trying to envision the potty, thoroughly convinced that I would be the owner of the "fur-lined" contraption. After much examination of what only my imagination could render, I finally decided that the rim would indeed be covered with fur. I never received that fur-lined potty and was not very disappointed. I thought I was so sneaky, hiding under that bed. I had been tricked by the very people of whom I had complete trust. Wait a minute. Had I not done the very same thing to them by hiding under the bed- food for thought?

Marcenia Hope

Giving Thanks

Sunday dinners were special, but there was no comparison to the anticipation of the holiday meals. I have admitted that as a child, Christmas was the highlight of my year. And furthermore, I must admit, well into my adulthood. The magic and charm were not however lost only on that one big day. Even back then, for me there was truly magic on Thanksgiving Day. It was the sweet surrender into the thrill of the season. Now, it is my favorite time of the year.

In my attic of memories, there is a shirtwaist dress, long sleeved for the weather, yet made of cotton print - cool for the hot kitchen. In its simple elegance, it rests on the shoulders of its owner - the Matriarch. The tendrils of loose hair touch the collar of the dress as they have escaped the bun that rests easily at the nape of her neck. Beads of perspiration collect on her face as she moves slowly and deliberately to accomplish the task at hand. There is a method and a rhythm in her assuredness, confidence born from years of practice. This is HER kitchen. This is her domain.

In the hub of this small, but sufficient kitchen, there sits the stove; laden with steaming pots, with smells emanating the air, filling every pore of the gray shotgun house on Fair Street. The laborious hours are too many to count, but the finale is at hand. Then, the slamming of the front screen door signifying that "we" have arrived echoing with a thunderous clap! We set our course for the kitchen, to inhale the most wonderful Thanksgiving smells, hoping erroneously that in doing so we will appease some of the hunger in the pit of our stomachs. Mimi turns; the Matriarch is now at full attention with a smile as big as the state of Georgia.

Hugs and kisses are swiftly executed as the men are "shooed" from the kitchen, leaving the women behind, me included, to assist in the final preparations of Thanksgiving Day. Notwithstanding her gentle command, my Daddy swipes a stalk of stuffed celery as he exits the room, leaving the Matriarch to suppress the smile, which hides behind the thin and pursed lips. It's his yearly tradition, a prelude to the experience of what Thanksgiving means to him, not only the scrumptious meal, but the junior varsity football game that he will attend shortly – The University of Georgia Bulldogs vs. the Georgia Tech Yellow Jackets.

The game will be played in downtown Atlanta at Bobby Dodd Stadium. The rivalry is fierce, but no less so than the one between my daddy and brother Billy who had decided at a young age to be a die-hard Georgia Tech fan. The atmosphere at the end of the day remains to be seen as the outcome of the game will surely affect each and every one of us left behind.

Thanksgiving for me was and still is the prelude to all things kind, good and human in the South. But, more importantly, it is in knowing that for the next few weeks, our world will turn to holiday celebrations and most importantly, the birth of Christ. Yes, there is another kick-off on this day that surely rivals the hearts of die- hard football fans everywhere - a more important one. It is the kick-off of what we all sometimes take for granted – thankfulness and blessings.

An Eye Opening Moment

Mimi died in the spring of her ninety third year. The sound of the front screen door as it was gently closed with reverence was a mockery of its usual clatter. There was no urgency to reach the confines of the house. Instead we all moved slowly and steadily toward the only room that would give us some comfort – the kitchen. It was spring, her favorite season, and the gravity of it held us all in a daze. How appropriate that she would leave us on a beautiful spring day! She loved all of God's creation. She not only loved flowers, she loved the trees. Mother has spoken of how she had an appreciation of the wind when it blew, making the leaves dance as if on parade, and her recognition of its value in God's perfect plan.

The sadness of the day hung over us like a pall there on Farris Avenue. My daddy, who had recently suffered his brain aneurysm and the repercussions of memory loss, sat with us around the kitchen table. He knew who we were, but was lost in the past, with no awareness of the present. Our hearts were heavy and there was very little conversation. There in the middle of the table were some Fig Newtons®. He picked up the fruited cookies and proceeded to offer one to each of us, calling us all by name and asking, "Would you like a Figaro®?" After his offer to us, he stopped his hand in front of himself and said, "Bill would you like a

Figaroo®?" It was an eye opening moment. We all looked at one another and laughed, and the pain of her loss was suspended for that instant, the first step in the long road to healing. Mimi loved my daddy, and he loved her as well, and they both would have loved the humor of that moment.

Mother wrote this poem in honor of Mimi not long after she died, in honor of her assent to heaven.

MARCH, 18 - 2000

Bye Bye Butterfly

Bye Bye Butterfly spread
your Beautiful wings And
fly, fly, fly, Right up To
the sky
Tell every twinkling
STAR Hello
dip your wings And
Soar High High High
As The sun winks its
Eye
And The fluffy clouds
drift By And the
Heavenly Music Rings
out As you Rest on
The Angel's Toes.
While the air smells
Soft As A Rose

I can only attribute one recipe in my repertoire to my grandmother, "Mimi". I never wrote down one word with a pencil or a pen. I just wrote her words of instruction in my heart and those words have been my guide throughout my life, both in and out of the kitchen. I do give tribute to Mimi for the one recipe that I know came from my great-great grandmother and it is cherished. This dish is from the mid to late 1800's. Since Mimi was born in 1903, I would estimate the time frame to be around the 1860's. I have never seen the recipe in any cookbook or tasted any yams like these. They are a favorite of my family and I only make them once a year - Thanksgiving. They are served at my table instead of the more traditional sweet potato casserole. The only reservation that I have in making them on Thanksgiving is the preparation time, which involves the manner in which they become the best yams known to man, at least to my family.

Be aware that the following recipe will not be found in any recipe book that hints of the word healthy. Of course the sweet potatoes themselves contain many healthy nutrients, but I would venture to say that any health benefit would quickly be negated, after they have been fried and then slowly cooked in butter and sugar, creating a most sinful syrup.

Candied Yams

3 to 4 lbs. of medium sweet potatoes (Choose potatoes that have skin that is reddish orange in color)
Mazola oil or peanut oil, your preference
1 to 2 sticks of margarine
1 c. granulated sugar

Place potatoes in very hot tap water to loosen the skin and make for easier peeling. Peel the potatoes. Cut into wedges of different sizes, down the length of the potato, making sure that the potatoes are a little less than a half inch thick, and not longer than about four inches. Do not cut the potatoes in a uniform fashion. The secret to their flavor lies in the shape of the potatoes. I have tried cutting them into round slices and the results are not the same.

You may deep fry or fry potatoes in an iron Dutch oven in about an inch of oil. Any Dutch oven will work. Bring the oil to medium high heat and add potatoes in a single layer, turning quickly, as they will brown very fast. Make sure the potatoes are light to dark brown, before removing them individually, then adding another batch of potatoes to the oil before it becomes too hot. Additional oil may be required, as the potatoes do absorb some of it. If you add more, make sure the temperature reaches a medium high before adding more potatoes. Continue the frying process until all of the potatoes are browned.

Once the potatoes have been fried, discard the oil, and add one stick of margarine to the Dutch oven. Place potatoes back in oven and sprinkle evenly with one cup of sugar. Cover immediately and reduce heat to low. Simmer for about 15 to 20 minutes, or until a syrup is formed. Do not stir the potatoes. Gently shift them with a spatula, until covered in syrup. Taste the potatoes and add more sugar if desired. (You may add additional butter and sugar, reducing the butter and sugar to half of the original proportions, i.e., ½ stick of margarine and ½ cup of sugar.) Once the syrup is melted, distinguish heat and allow to rest on burner until ready to serve. You may warm on medium heat just before serving.

The Kitchen Beckons

My kitchen adventures would be plentiful as I began my teen years. There was no hesitation on my mother's part to allow me free reign in what was her domain. She welcomed my presence and fostered my love for cooking, and I am sure the pleasure was all hers, as it must have been a treat for her. Her praises were so gratifying and I craved more and more of them. It was a win –win situation for both of us.

By the age of thirteen, my ventures in the kitchen had begun on a regular basis. Chocolate fudge was my specialty. The recipe came from the box of Hershey's cocoa and you better believe that it was the best you could make. None of that marshmallow fudge for me, I made the good stuff. I had it down to a science. My daddy loved it too, and I would make it especially for him. I remember standing at the cooktop, looking through the bar opening into the den. My daddy would brag profusely when I made his favorite. I would profess that I had made it just for him, secretly craving the sugary sweet, chocolate delight. I am sure now he was on to me, but he never let on.

In my high school years, I continued to find my way into the kitchen more and more often. I loved cooking for my family, even though my brothers enjoyed teasing me when things did not turn out as I had anticipated.

I recall the first time I washed a chicken for preparation. I was at home alone and mother had called to ask me to begin preparing our supper. Supper, as discussed earlier was the evening meal at our home. I must have washed the chicken for at least an hour. I see myself now, standing at the kitchen sink of stainless steel. I remember picking out the feather stubs that had been left, thinking I had outsmarted the butcher in my inspection. Mother had taught me that a chicken needed to be washed thoroughly. Again in my effort to be the perfectionist, I went to the extreme. That was some dirty bird!

Through those years, I cooked almost everything. I fried chicken, cooked peas and butterbeans like a true southern woman. I watched my mother and learned the skills used to create a meal. Timing each dish to be ready for serving simultaneously with other dishes doesn't just happen. The art of perfecting recipes for easy delivery takes practice and my mother was a master. It all starts with preparing the dish that takes the longest to cook first, then working your way through the other items on the menu. We did not always have the perfect presentation in my home on a day to day basis, but it did not matter. What mattered was the family time around our table that was priceless and the food that was memorable.

Sometimes we had fresh flowers gracing the table, that mother had picked. Many were simple and the honeysuckle that grew wild was a favorite. For Mother's Day, Jan and I would pick fresh flowers and have them on the table for breakfast. We would get up early and cook the meal for her. It was our tradition, one that I continued for many years after I married.

By the age of fifteen, my repertoire included many southern dishes, but I was interested in preparing other dishes as well. Our birthday celebrations were a chance for me to show off my skills. On one occasion I prepared my specialty - lasagna and carrot cake. I was such a romantic at heart and also wanted to create the perfect atmosphere - by candlelight. Imagine my hurt when my father refused to eat my Italian specialty by the glow of candles, insisting on turning on the lights. It was the demeanor of the men of that generation, they were to be respected and feared, but loved. Maybe he was just a little uncomfortable and was struggling to accept that his daughter had romantic ideas. Better yet, perhaps it was the absence of biscuits or cornbread that caused his disgruntled behavior!

My Carrot Cake was loved by my immediate family. I can vividly remember sitting at the kitchen table grating the carrots that I used in the cake. I don't remember how much of the grated carrot that was needed for the recipe, but it was a task that I found unpleasant. Invariably, I would end up grating my knuckle and I would have to stop and allow my mother to finish the task. I later mastered the grater, learning to quit long before the carrot became too short to grate. Then, there were the nuts that I had to shell. Pecans were and remain a southern staple in many baked goods. We were lucky enough to have several trees on our property. I would have to crack and remove the meat for the cup of nuts required for the icing. Would there ever be a cake made in this day and age, if the preparation for the ingredients were as difficult to achieve? My cake was worth a mint when I got through, but the compliments from my family were worth more than a mint to me.

I still have memories of a certain carrot cake that never was – eaten that is! I started dating a young man, but only for a short time. He was in college, but also enlisted in the Army Reserves. Just as we started dating he was sent to basic training. He loved carrot cake and he requested that I make one for him. There was a slight problem. He was in Arizona!

His request was for a carrot cake did not go unanswered. I went to the Post Office to see how long it would take to ship the cake to Arizona and I was told three days. I made the cake and never even gave it a second thought that it would need to be refrigerated; after all it had cream cheese icing on it. It seemed like such a good idea at the time. The cake arrived two weeks later! He admitted that the cake was a mess. Cream cheese icing can't take a three day journey, without refrigeration, much less two weeks! Imagine his embarrassment when he opened the cake. Imagine my embarrassment when I realized what a fool I had been.

To Cook and to Cherish

Not only did I enjoy cooking a meal, I wanted my presentation to be a reflection of graciousness. I also wanted to learn to entertain properly. I admired the cherished ritual of sipping tea and eating dainty foods that accompanied them. I was and have always been attracted to table linens, beautiful dishes and anything that can make a meal special. One of the favorite excursions that my mother made sure that I was able to experience was the luncheon at *Rich's Department Store* in the *Magnolia Room*. The wonderful chicken salad, frozen fruit salad and cheese straws were my favorite, their specialty and a classic.

Rich's had a fashion show during the luncheon hour. I recall being in awe of the lovely ladies sporting the latest fashions. The experience served me well as I found myself wanting to duplicate the special memory. In later years, I created my own version of the infamous *Magnolia Room* specialty. My motto now is, "If there is not a special occasion to celebrate – make one." I still feel special each and every time I duplicate the *Magnolia Room's* classic for friends and family. In the south, a bridal shower is not a shower without chicken salad – any way you serve it.

No Regrets

Community College was my choice after I graduated from high school. I traveled twenty five miles every day and then returned to work in a clothing store in our town. I wanted to major in Interior Design, because I loved beautiful home furnishings and decorating, almost as much as I loved to cook. As it happened, the only home I would decorate was my own and sooner than I imagined.

After two years of working and attending college, I had dated a few guys that I had met in the clothing store. I dated a hunk, a lawyer and an accountant. The hunk could kiss, but could not carry on a conversation. The lawyer was on the fast track to the bedroom, after a lunch at the Burger King – not a chance! The accountant gave my family his dog because he could no longer keep it at his apartment. My dad met him for the first time and made sure that he told him I could cook. His phone calls were numerous, the date numbered one, and that was one too many for me.

I soon fell in love, but not with a college acquaintance, instead my employer's son. I didn't mean for it to happen, but it did. I got married at age twenty, just a baby by today's standards, but I have no regrets and Ronnie is still the love of my life. I only went to college for two years, but I got my education in the business world and life in general. I continued on with my schooling in the art of cooking, because I was lucky enough to marry a man whose family loved and cherished cooking.

Transformation

Those tender years, I had been inspired, not only with the art of cooking, but with the satisfaction and rewards that it could bring. I began my married life with meager tools of the trade. My wedding gifts were inclusive of the standard kitchen tools and I was thrilled that I could call them my own.

There are some things that just can't be bought and one of those was Mimi's priceless gift of her rolling pin with red handles. I have never owned another and feel it would be blasphemous to replace it. I recently saw a smaller version of the standard rolling pin, but resisted the temptation to add it to my kitchen wares. Thoughts of the wooden pin with its worn red handles, each one holding scars of labor and memories of the love gift, caused me to dismiss entertaining the idea of a new one.

Years before, the rolling pin had been borrowed by my mother from Mimi and then returned to her. I don't know at what age, but I was told that when I witnessed Mimi using it, I proclaimed, "That's my mother's rolling pin!" Imagine the swell of my heart, when she presented it to me as a wedding gift. Imagine my heart each time I reach for it and touch the wood, feeling my Mimi's presence, keeping her legacy alive. Back then, armed with my rolling pin and eager to learn more, I had the techniques and the knowledge, but not the experience to be the cook I aspired to be, and certainly not the wife and mother that I would become. I would be studious and watchful and I would listen to my new instructors. Each day would be a classroom and I was a willing student. I would be transformed.

Miss Winnie

I can only imagine Winnie Garrett Bennett as she removed her pound cake from the oven, a staple in her kitchen. She must have felt a great sense of pride as she had built her reputation as always having one baked and ready to serve. Coupled with the frozen ice cream that she made and placed in ice trays for the freezer, she was prepared for both the expected and unexpected guests. She proudly served the cake on her beautiful cut glass saucers, with a sherbet glass in the center to hold the prized frozen delight – her trademark. That was her claim to fame.

There is at least one in every family, and sometimes many more. Yes, the one who can walk in a room and the conversation stops mid-stream. It's not her tilted chin or her winsome smile. All eyes rest on the package in her hands. Her culinary expertise is brimming and flowing over, as watchful eyes try to guess what she has cooked for the occasion. Surely it must be their favorite. More than likely it will be, because her reputation has been built on it. Yes, there is one in every family. It may be a wife, mother or an aunt, but the love is felt by all when the prize is revealed.

It was not unlike this scenario for Winnie. She was from a middle class generation that took pride in their domestic accomplishments. For most of those middle class women of that era, their very reputation and certainly their respect was measured by their expertise in the kitchen. Now that women have been liberated, the tradition remains, but the emphasis has deteriorated. Are women better off than before? I would have to say no to the person who has never had a home cooked meal, delivered from one of those women held in high esteem. I would have to say yes to the woman who is still enslaved to the kitchen, who does not stand beside her husband, but behind him.

Frankly, I am more than buttermilk, eggs and cornmeal. I wish to be respected for my accomplishments, as I suspect the women of that era were tenacious in their domestication, but equally so in their need for respect as individuals.

Winnie was born in the late nineteenth century and lived through the era of women's suffrage as it culminated in 1920's. She and her family lived in Middle Georgia and farmed for a living. The mother of four sons and one daughter, she would live to see the loss of two of her sons, one at a very young age and the other in his twenties. Her daughter was the only girl of that generation - females would not be in the cards for the next generation, as six Bennett boys were born, one of those my future husband. Winnie was my husband's paternal grandmother – Grandma Bennett.

I certainly did not realize or recognize the implication of marrying a man whose entire generation was barren of females. It did occur to me that once I was pregnant for the first time, I was teetering on the brink of girl-less-ness after delivering my first son. Needless to say, when my daughter was born, groggy from the clouds of anesthesia from surgery, upon my first reaction to the news of my daughter, I remarked, "A girl, a real girl?" Yes, she was real and I waited nine months to discover her identity. My heart already knew who SHE was before she was born, but I would not reveal it to my mind.

I never had the pleasure of meeting Grandma Bennett. I do know that she was a staunch Baptist. So staunch that after her death, when a family member implied anything that would be outside the realm of Baptist conventions, remarks would be made, "If Winnie knew that, she would turn over in her grave!" That has been food for thought of what her opinion of me would have been. Would she appreciate my love of cooking and the fact that I use many of her recipes and techniques that were passed down to me through her daughter-in-law, Mary Frances – now that's a southern name! Would she appreciate the fact that I enjoy using her phrase when I am complimented on the food I have cooked? As recanted to me, when someone praised the food she prepared, she would reply, "That's the kind I make!" I may have never met her, but sometimes I feel her very presence especially when I cook a pound cake. Grandma Bennett died when my husband was twelve.

One of my treasured pieces of glassware is a gift from my mother-in-law Mary Frances. She gave me Grandma Bennett's punch bowl and the set of glass saucers with matching sherbet dishes she lovingly used. There must have been countless times, that the saucers were used to serve her famed pound cake, along with the ice cream in the glasses. I picture her guests on the porch with nothing in mind, but the sheer joy of consuming her confection, getting lost in frozen thoughts and the dense texture of her cake.

I think of Grandma each and every time I use the glassware. Her cake and ice cream were her legend. To serve them on the glassware defined her. She was gracious and kind, as evidenced by her presentation. When using a sentimental piece, one that has a story, you are able to convey to the recipient how much you honor their company. Who cares about having to wash all of those special dishes by hand? I will not cheat myself of the food I have prepared to rest on a paper plate, even for every day meals. Pass the *Corning Ware®* please, and make it French!

Grandma and Granddaddy Bennett

Mary Ella

Mary Ella Miller was my husband's maternal grandmother, born in 1909, married at the age of eighteen to Millard Lyman Jones. Lyman had a pulpwood business and Mary Ella taught school while raising her family. They were the epitome of hard working middle class who strove to provide a college education to each and every one of their children. Mary Ella's legacy as the matriarch of her family began at age twenty when she gave birth to Mary Frances, the oldest of six children and who would later become my mother-in-law. I became a part of their family when I married her son Ronnie at age twenty.

Mary and Lyman were affectionately known to their grandchildren as "MaMa" and "DeDaddy". Little did I know that I had married the golden grandchild, the favorite of "MaMa". It was all a farce. She did not love Ronnie any more than she loved any of the rest of her nineteen grandchildren, plus the newly acquired one. But, she sure enjoyed perpetuating the idea that he was her favorite. She did not have anyone fooled; her love was abundant and apparent to all she loved and those who loved her.

Just a few short weeks after my marriage, MaMa and DeDaddy were house sitting for Ronnie's parents who had gone out of town. We were invited to dinner. I wanted to show off my cooking skills, so I assisted in the kitchen. My contribution was a lemon pie. I knew the recipe ingredients by heart, but unfortunately not the right measurements. That little tidbit can be helpful when baking! A little pinch of this and little pinch of that can work many times. That particular time, I added the fresh lemon juice to the pie mixture, without a measurement, confident in my memorization skills. I had grown up watching my mother and Mimi adding ingredients to dishes, never measuring them.

The pie looked delicious and I was satisfied with my work. I cut a slice and served it to DeDaddy, waiting for a reaction. He had no control. Both sides of his cheeks caved in, his mouth protruding to form what looked like a kiss. He nodded his head, a motion that proclaimed to me that the pie was good. I took my first bite and felt my cheeks involuntarily surrender in defeat as the surge of sour taste was followed by an uncontrolled frown. At that point, there was more pie on my face than in my mouth!

We all had a good laugh, as my blunder was quite obvious to everyone. I chalked that one up to experience. I learned that baking usually requires precise measurement. MaMa never said a word, not one. She knew that I had learned from my mistake. In the future, she was always a gentle teacher when I had the opportunity to watch her in the kitchen. It was not often, but each and every experience was priceless.

MaMa spoiled her children, grandchildren and family. She took great pride in the food she prepared. Could she know that her little tricks of the trade could spoil future generations? It was her habit to make cream style corn - her way. She started the custom of cutting the corn from the cob, by splitting each grain down the center first, beginning from one end of the corn and gently slicing the center of each row with the tip of her knife. Then she would slice the corn from top to bottom, cutting three to four rows at a time, removing about three fourths of the kernels, careful not to cut all the way down to the cob. The corncob would then be rotated in a circular motion, as her knife would make a final scrape of the cob to extract the "milk" and the starch that makes the corn produce a creamy texture when cooked. The technique of splitting the kernels through the center takes more time and patience, especially when preparing it in bulk for the freezer. The corn was originally made this way, so that the younger children could digest it easily, but the texture was also recognized as superior to the entire family. It takes a little more work, but worth the effort!

MaMa, not unlike Grandma Bennett made her mark in the kitchen. She was known, among many other favorites, for her cakes and fried apple pies. It was not unusual for her to fry enough pies to fill a large platter for a church gathering and of course, upon family requests. The pies were made of dried apples that had been cooked and sweetened to just the right taste. Oh to have one right now! I can cook them, but somehow they are just not the same.

Mama lived until three months shy of her ninety ninth birthday. It was a hot August day and the miles turned to eternity on I-16, the destination to her final resting place, appearing to elude us as we drove down the desolate highway in Middle Georgia. Finally, we reached our exit, only to face another stretch of interminable miles that would soon take us to the little white church and cemetery where MaMa would be laid to rest. The sign on the little stretch of dirt road that lay in front of the church read Sudie Pearl Jones – named for the great-grandmother of my husband. She had changed her name from Shelly Pearl to Sudie Pearl early on in life, because she disliked the name Shelly so much. The church was named Cedar Grove United Methodist. The double doors would soon be opened wide, an invitation to those who would pay their last respects to Mary Ella Miller Jones and to reveal a quaint sanctuary, sparsely, but regally furnished. A funeral service had been held in North Carolina, her home for the past ten years. This would be a reunion of sorts, for she was finally coming home, for her interment.

Mary Ella lay in state as close friends and relatives from the small community that represented her roots, gathered in the church to give her a last goodbye. I was touched by one of the family's caregivers who literally jumped up and down in glee as she saw my husband for the first time in at least forty years; the sound of heels popping on the heart pine wooden floor proclaimed that "Junebug" had made her entrance. Now in her seventies, she reminisced of her days of changing, not only my husband's diaper, but many diapers for the family that had eventually expanded from six children to some fifty six grandchildren and great-grandchildren combined.

Junebug was a legend in that family, loved and revered, for she was family indeed. She was there to honor a woman who knew no color during the turbulent times of racial tensions. She was there along with the widowed wife of Boots, a man also of color whom MaMa and DeDaddy had raised as their own, both there to pay their respects to her. Boots had been given a home at the age of eight and given the college education of his choice by a family that chose humanity.

As introductions were made to friends and family of the past, I turned my attention to the tiny little woman whose years had robbed her of her stature. She was somewhat frail; however, her ninety three years still yielded her a sound mind. I was the witness to the final kiss Aunt Alene gave MaMa in that tiny little country church fondly called Cedar Grove. My heart was full and the tears flowed freely as the glimpse of those sisters and the short mortality of life was revealed. It was a humbling experience, to say the least, feeling the embrace of sisterhood as I have never felt it before, knowing the vulnerabilities of life yet to come. MaMa had given so much and taken so little, this grand lady who had graced the earth for some ninety nine years, just shy of a century. We had her so long, but life never seems long enough, and for her sister who was ninety three, not long enough of that I'm sure.

Friends and family that spoke of her at MaMa's graveside all shared the same underlying message that conveyed the joy she always brought when preparing their favorite food. The final words all echoed the same message and were a proclamation of her long and prosperous life, as a wife, mother and grandmother. We still miss you MaMa.

MaMa and DeDaddy

Many of MaMa's recipes have filtered down indirectly to me through her daughter, my mother-in-law. The most famous in her repertoire was her recipe for fried apple pies-as written in her own words, followed by a favorite roll recipe. By no means, do the selections begin to encompass her expertise in cooking.

Fried Apple Pies

8 oz. dried apples
2 cups water
2 cups of sugar

Cook apples and water in a large boiler, bring to a boil. Reduce heat and simmer for 30 to 40 minutes or until apples are tender and can be mashed with a vegetable masher. Add sugar and cook for 10 to 15 minutes (until apples are thick). Set aside and let cool.

PASTRY

3 cups self-rising flour
2/3 c. milk
1/3 c. oil (I use Mazola® for pastry and frying)

Combine ingredients as any pastry (you may have to add more flour to handle). Divide dough in 2 parts. Use part on floured wax paper and pat out to about 1 inch thick and cut out with a large biscuit cutter. (I pinch off pieces with my hand the size of a biscuit) Then roll out as thin as you can handle, 5 or 6 inch circle. Put 2 tablespoons of cooked apples on 1 side of circle, and then moisten edge of pastry with your fingers dipped in cold water. Fold over other half of pastry, being sure edges are even; then take a fork or finger, put in flour and press pastry edges together firmly.

Heat oil in electric fry pan to about 375 degrees. Cook pies until golden brown on both sides, turning only once. Drain on paper towel.

Yeast Muffin Surprise

4 c. self-rising flour
1/4 c. sugar
1/2 c. very warm water
1 envelope active dry yeast
1 ½ c. milk
2 sticks of margarine

In a medium size microwavable bowl, melt margarine on high for 1 minute. Remove from microwave. In a small mixing bowl, mix yeast with warm water until dissolved. Stir with a wire whisk into the melted margarine until evenly distributed. Add the milk and stir until well blended. Blend in flour and sugar, stirring to form a soft dough that resembles a very thick batter. Dough will appear somewhat lumpy. Drop by heaping tablespoons into greased muffin tin until half full. Bake on 400 degrees for 15 to 20 minutes until golden brown. Yields 24 muffins.

*I frequently cut this recipe in half to serve for evening meals. You may make the entire recipe and store the remaining dough in the refrigerator for 2 to 3 days.

Mary Frances

Mary Frances Jones was born in 1929, the oldest of a family of six children, daughter to Mary Ella and Lyman Jones. She was also the oldest of five girls who enjoyed her appointed station in life by birth and certainly exercised her right as the big sister. It is my understanding, that it was not easy being one of the sisters of Mary Frances, since she was the first child in the Jones family and the first grandchild on both sides of her family. She was famously spoiled.

It has been reported that as a young lady, Mary Frances was a perfectionist in her appearance. Her clothes were kept crisply ironed and her shoes were always polished and no sister dared to borrow them; at least not without her knowledge. I am also told that one of her sisters borrowed her shoes once without permission and the repercussions were not worth the dare. After all, she had a shoe size of five and her sister's larger foot must have wreaked havoc on those borrowed shoes. Those sisters towed the line, at least where her personal belongings were concerned.

Mary Frances would become an exceptional cook and held in the highest esteem by all the members of her family for her abilities in the kitchen. Over the years whenever she has visited her sisters, she could not escape her obligation. Their kitchen would become her domain, waiting for her arrival. Great and wonderful food has abounded in both hers and the kitchens of her siblings and she relished their accolades. Each one of them and their children likewise have had their favorite requests for her to prepare and she has always tried to fill their order, however tall it might be. Mary Frances has been a cook, chef and a food connoisseur in her own right, but most importantly – a beloved daughter and sister.

Mary Frances became the wife of Ernest Bennett and was married for over thirty five years and counting their courtship, his beloved for over thirty nine. He died at the age of fifty five, leaving her a young widow. She met him at church when she was only fourteen. They dated for four years and married immediately after high school. Their honeymoon was spent at his sister's home, vacated for them for one night. Their humble beginnings only allowed for them to reside with his parents, until after the birth of their first son. It was so much more economical in the forties and fifties to live with extended family and certainly acceptable. She has never married again and considered herself always married to her first and only love, Ernest.

Mary Frances and Ernest

Mary Frances has always been known to me as Mrs. Bennett, since she was first my employer. I have never changed the salutation and still garner her that respect, but will reference her as Mary Frances. As I said before, calling an elder by their first name has never been the southern way and in her case I defer to the code of graciousness.

When Mary Frances became my mother-in-law in 1974, I did not realize just how much her expertise in the kitchen would mean to me. Two families had merged and so had two methods of cooking the very same food. Over the years, I have taken the best of both and formed some of my own techniques and recipes. She has shared so many recipes with me and has been a very important influence of how and what I cook today. Most importantly, her instructions have made the greatest impact.

When I first started observing Mary Frances, I was surprised to learn that Middle Georgians and North Georgians could have a completely different way to prepare food. It was a tug of war, trying to learn new ways of cooking and pleasing a husband that was just glad to have a wife that could cook. Now that was a commodity as a newlywed. I felt sure that every one of my friends had the same opportunities to learn to cook. Surely all girls were trained in the kitchen as I had been, but I soon learned that was not the case.

How lucky I and her family members have all been to have Mary Frances as a teacher. We did not have to gather our knowledge from instructions in cook books. She had done that for us, soaking up every word that she had read, and then giving us all personal instruction. Her collection of cookbooks would rival any other.

Back then, I was eager to learn new techniques and recipes as a newlywed. Mary Frances was eager to share. There have been few conversations over the course of thirty nine years with her that have not included a discussion of cooking. Each and every time she had picked up a magazine or a newspaper; she had found an opportunity to read about food or cooking. Snippets of advice have come regularly for me. Mary Frances has given me countless hours of instruction. A lifetime of living the American dream of home and family, with visions of the generations to come was halted for her on a warm spring day and the months to follow were painful and heart wrenching for us. Mary Frances suffered a major mind and life altering stroke.

Stamped in Blue Ink

Just after the stroke and with the seriousness of the outcome, I found myself cleaning the house of Mary Frances. Her new place of residence would be a nursing home. Her house was almost a shrine to the art of cooking. The recipes abounded, books and books, some clipped from magazines, but my favorite, the ones in her own handwriting. They were found on the backs of bank deposit slips, the inside of cookbook covers, numbering in the hundreds. She silently spoke to me at every turn when I entered the kitchen; the evidence of her absence was obvious. Cleaning and organizing her home was one of the hardest things that I have ever done, knowing she would not be back. The food items would need to go. It was long and laborious, painful to say the least.

I began to clean out the cabinets. There I spotted it on the top shelf, as if it was left there for me to find. It was staring at me with a familiarity that only my eyes would recognize - a box of Hershey's ® Cocoa. It was not just a box of cocoa; it was a very old box, made of tin. My hands were shaking and my knees felt weak as I reached for that box. It was taller and more slender than the newer boxes today. I examined it, turning it over in my hand. My eyes spied a stamp on the bottom of the box. The price was stamped in blue ink $.47- forty seven cents. I could not believe my eyes, and as I turned the can to the back side, I trembled in anticipation. There it was - the recipe for the chocolate fudge that I had so proudly made for my daddy, the recipe that no longer existed on the newer cans. I am sure that I could have retrieved that recipe from the internet, but I had not made the effort. My discovery was far better. It was real and very tangible, resting there in my sweating hand. I slowly climbed down, relaying my discovery to the friend who was helping me with my task - the story of how I had cooked homemade fudge for my daddy.

How ironic it was to find that box of cocoa. It was so relevant, but yet so irrelevant to anyone, but me. What was the correlation? My father had lived in the past for the last years of his life, one I had adored, and one I had made fudge for - from the

110

recipe on that same type container that I used when I was only twelve years old! Mary Frances had just passed over the threshold of reality and surely her demise from the kitchen forever. It was too much for me to digest at the moment, I could only feel a loss of not one, but two. I took the can and its contents, my new found treasure, and held it with reverence. I knew where its new home would be. It rests on the top shelf of my kitchen cabinet and there it will stay.

The Victor of Near and Dear

After that fateful Spring Day, days turned into weeks and weeks to months. Soon the winter months were upon us. Rushing from work on a cold and wet wintry day, skies full of promise of impending snow; I sought solace in the meal that I planned for dinner, to get me through the visit to the nursing home. It is never pleasant to go there and if many days pass, it becomes harder to return. Yet, on this day I felt beckoned to give hope and promise to Mary Frances who resides behind the walls of endless days and many times, sleepless nights.

I would be making chicken stew and cornbread for supper. While growing up, many churches in our region had chicken stew suppers as fund raisers and some still do. The stew was made at home, and then transported where it was served for a donation to benefit the church. The ladies of the church also made wonderful desserts to complete a most satisfying meal. On this day, the threat of a cold winter night brought back memories of that gratifyingly warm dish.

Mary Frances shares her stories during our visit and I listen attentively to give support to them – never giving her a hint that the world in which she exists only belongs to her. I silently mock the stroke, as she unlocks her mind and reveals to me some of her treasured secrets, knowing at that moment that she is the victor of all that was near and dear to her. Even though the stroke took away her ability to physically prepare food, it cannot rob her of the wonderful hints and instructions that she has used for so many years. They are secure and not surprisingly, each story she tells includes food preparation.

The domain in which Mary Frances lives knows no time.

Yet, her state of mind is a gift. It's a gift that lightens our hearts and minds as we walk away each time, knowing that she has found anew, a life that transcends her helpless state, both physically and mentally. The stroke has robbed her of ability to walk and the use of her left arm. It was mean and spiteful and robbed her of her capacity to live alone. She recognizes her family and has limited short term memory, but in conversation she will slip quietly away into her own world of friends and family, some that have long been dead.

God has been merciful and has given her joy and happiness, and she has kept her sense of humor that creates laughter from both residents and the staff. I know that whenever I need to be grounded, I can stop by and as painful as it is to see her in her helpless state, I can come away restored. That is her gift to me.

On this day, we laughed and joked as she ate the fast food that I had picked up as a treat, a reprieve from the monotonous food prepared on the premises. When our visit came to an end, I spoke of my plans to prepare the chicken stew and cornbread, feeling guilty that I could not offer her a place at my table. She asked if I would be back and I did not promise, after all, the weather is nasty and it is so cold outside. I did promise, however, to return "tomorrow".

It was a three hour ordeal, from the time I left the nursing home to prepare the meal. I had to stop at the grocery and purchase the ingredients, then drive home to prepare the stew. My heart strings were tugging and by the time I finished the stew and the cornbread that I knew she loved so dearly, I was resolute in my mission to deliver the goods.

When I arrived at the nursing home, she was already lying down, eyes closed, but not asleep. I cajoled her into opening her eyes with the promise of cornbread and stew. As soon as I got her into a sitting position, with eyes closed she tasted the bread. The reward for me had to be far more satisfying, than how good the cornbread tasted to her. My treasured chicken stew was enjoyed as well, but the cornbread took top honors as she spoke eloquently about how much she enjoyed it, somewhere lost in words that only she could access and spend like gold as she granted them to me. I felt full of emotion and motionless as I as I tried to depart the premises, feeling full, yet empty. The mean stroke had won, but she persevered for five years, bringing joy in her new home to residents and staff alike.

Chicken Stew

3 to 4 lb. fryer
2 to 3 qts. water
3 ribs celery hearts, sliced thin
1 large carrot, julienned
1 tsp. black pepper
1 tsp. salt
2 c. half and half
½ stick margarine

Thickener
½ c. plain flour
1 c. water
Stir together with a whisk until smooth.

Wash chicken and place in a 4 qt. stock pot with enough water to just cover the bird. Add salt and pepper. Bring to a boil. Reduce heat to simmer and cover. Simmer for 1 to ½ hours, until the breast is fork tender. Remove bird from stock pot and debone, tearing the meat into bite size pieces. Place the chicken back into the chicken broth, add vegetables. Bring to a boil on high heat. Reduce heat and cook 20 minutes to tender the vegetables. While cooking, make thickener and set aside. Add butter to chicken and vegetables, and then slowly add half and half, increasing the heat to medium high. When the stew starts to bubble, remove from heat. Slowly add the thickener to desired consistency. Continue stirring until smooth. Spoon into bowls and serve with saltines. Cornbread is also delicious with the stew.

*If you prefer white meat, add 4 bone-in breasts to the stock pot with the chicken and discard the dark meat. The fryer provides a richer stock for the stew, unlike boneless breasts.

The recipes of Mary Frances are many and their origin sometimes forgotten, but never the lips that spoke them or her words in that deliberate penmanship that branded them with love when written. Some found their home on snippets of paper, nonetheless they remain cherished and I honor and feel privileged to share one of her most cherished recipes.

Pecan Pie

Pre-heat oven to 325 degrees.

3 c. whole pecans
1 c. light corn syrup
1 c. light brown sugar
6 eggs
Pinch of salt
1 stick of butter
3 unbaked pie shells (Do not use deep dish)

In a medium size mixing bowl, cream butter and sugar with an electric mixer. Add corn syrup and blend well, then add eggs one at a time, beating well after each addition. Stir in nuts, vanilla and salt. Spoon mixture into pie shells. Bake for 50 minutes or until a toothpick comes out clean when inserted into the center.

Aunt Rea

The first time that I met Marie, who was called "Aunt Rea," by her nieces and nephews was while I worked for the Bennett's in their clothing store. I immediately recognized the sorrow in her face, even at my young age. She was widowed in her early forties, and that was followed two years later by another life crushing blow - the death of a son. She was the only sister of my father-in-law. Prim and proper as a lady could be, I recognized in her, the same traits many of my school teachers possessed. Their lives were governed by the same discipline that they garnered in the classroom. She was indeed a reflection of those same ladies from my childhood - ladies who were impeccable in their dress. Her clothes were always neatly pressed as was her hair and makeup always in place. She had taught school before raising her family. There is just something special about those who choose to teach children, especially not their own. They seem to embody discipline, both inside and outside the classroom.

My first visit to Aunt Rea's home was some thirty odd years ago. Aunt Rea lived in the small Middle Georgia town of Eastman on a quiet street with a perfectly manicured lawn. The town was quite flat in my estimation. Being a girl who had lived all of her life on the outskirts of the North Georgia Mountains, the quaint little flat town was charming and more like the small towns I had seen on television. The house had a car port, unlike the more traditional closed garages of today. The area was immaculate. It was a temporary respite for a hot afternoon and its chairs offered the opportunity to sit for a visit, or more often than not, shell a bushel of peas. It felt comfy and downright lazy to sit there in the quiet little Middle Georgia town, if the heat had not been so unbearable.

The humidity was at the normal summer high level that would make the space above a person's upper lip transform into a mustache of sweat – not very attractive when trying to make a good impression. And the gnats. What can I say about those black little vermin who swarm around a person's face as if they are attached by invisible tentacles that practically form a veil? A constant swat of the wrist could only create a short lived reprieve from the gnats and their mission; in my assessment, if continued on a regular basis, carpal tunnel syndrome would surely set in. The sweat only served to draw them nearer and closer to their prey.

Once inside Aunt Rea's home, the heat and gnats were easy to forget. The smells of a wonderful lunch can do that to you. The lady peas on the menu were a product of hours of preparation, since they were fresh and had to be shelled. They were the staple of this Middle Georgia town, as I was soon to learn. It was not uncommon for Aunt Rea to have a couple of bushels preserved in her freezer.

I soon spied the pound cake on the counter. I learned that there would always be one freshly made, waiting to be devoured. Just like her mother Winnie before her, the cake was her trademark. She made potato salad on that day and I was amazed that it could be prepared and served in a much smaller quantity that the five pounds my mother was accustomed to making for the holidays. Potato salad had always been made in large quantities in my family and reserved for special occasions. I changed my perspective that day.

The kitchen was small, but adequate. Aunt Rea had a place for everything; each and every inch was used to the maximum. The color in the kitchen was yellow and it was home to a big soft yellow refrigerator. It was a Frigidaire®. At that time, it had already passed its life expectancy, but it continued to hum along and stood in its austerity, daring its owner to remove it from the kitchen.

As the years passed, and visits were made to that yellow kitchen, the refrigerator continued to reign. It was always a treat for my husband to see, knowing that it had far surpassed the expectations of its owner. He teased her that he wanted it when she decided to purchase a new one, if it was still working. Then one day, Aunt Rea replaced it. She moved it in the outside storage and it held cold bottled Cokes®, until the day she died. It was ours for the taking, but in our home, it would not be the same. Aunt Rea was gone and the fascination for the yellow refrigerator as well.

The Hill

Our first home was an apartment on a hill. As I was slowly being transformed into a married woman, all my dreams and aspirations of being a good wife and mother were beginning to become a reality. You don't just go from being single one day, and then married the next, without going through some growing pains, but we survived rather nicely. I began with the old fashioned idea that the wife was the cook and caretaker of the home, exercising my mothering instincts on my husband, as most southern women of my generation. I found no resistance. He was, and still is, spoiled. I've liberated myself somewhat over the years, but it has been a hard habit to break. When you first get married, all of a sudden you are part of a team with responsibilities that don't just include your own well-being. I was in charge of my own kitchen and it felt good. I cooked everything in the apartment on the hill in that kitchen that was a 6X12 galley style, a laboratory of experimentation.

I tried lots of new recipes in those years, even buying an upright freezer that took a big chunk out of the limited workspace. I tried my hand at freezing vegetables and was quite successful, garnering the respect of some of the other residents. We even bought fresh beef for our freezer. The aforementioned women in my life would play a great role in the shaping of my skills and ideas. My aspirations of becoming a good cook and being recognized for my achievements were my goal. I was eager to add the title to my name in my new family. My family had given me the confidence I needed to begin my journey, but I was in for a bumpy ride.

Was I seeking fame in the kitchen outside of the praises from my family? I would have to say yes, a sense of validation lingering somewhere from childhood, a need to be fulfilled. I dreamed of entertaining someday on a grand scale, complete with tables covered in linens and fine vases of flowers. I treasured the advice from my Aunt Jean, "There is so much more to creating a wonderful meal – atmosphere". I wanted atmosphere to play an important role when I entertained, so no matter how large or how small, I worked to achieve it, as much as I did in preparing a meal.

At the time, I thought that cooking a full course meal was

perfectly normal for young wives my age, unaware of just how rare it was even then for a young wife in the 1970's, to cook as well as our mothers; I mastered the kitchen in those early years on the hill. I cannot say that I did not make any mistakes and I occasionally burned or over cooked a dish. The worst problem I had was in reducing the amount of food I prepared for a family of six to just the two of us.

My first attempt at duplicating the menu from *Richs Magnolia Room's* luncheon specialty, that I so adored, was almost successful. However, I burned the bottoms of my rendition of their cheese straws. I was far from humiliation, but definitely embarrassed in the presence of my humble guests; young housewives with no aspirations of impending grandeur.

A Perfect Day

It was a long five years on the hill. Our apartment building was the host to eight families. Residents came and went, bonds were made and some neighbors became lifelong friends. We wanted a house so bad! We also knew that you had to crawl before you walk, but that was not very comforting as our stay on the hill seemed like forever. It was not what we had in mind. Living in our first apartment extended far longer that we had ever expected.

In the beginning, I had been so excited to be married that it did not matter, but as time moved on, the apartment life became more and more confining. There was however, the camaraderie of the wonderful neighbors that shared our building. There were those who now seem a distant memory in our life, but some that have never left our hearts. Those are the kind of people that you may never see for months or maybe years, but upon seeing them again, you feel as though time has stood still.

Friendships were forged and memories of those days still bring a smile and sometimes, even a giggle. One of our first Christmas tree hunting adventures is the source of more than a smile. When relived, it is the compilation of warm and tender thoughts, coupled with an adrenalin rush instantaneously making me shiver with sheer pleasure. It is like capturing a butterfly in the palm of your hand, feeling the gentle rustle of the wings, knowing that its release is eminent, yet savoring its tender presence.

One Sunday afternoon as Christmas was impending, Ronnie and I, our neighbors, along with their three month old daughter, climbed into the '64 Chevrolet pickup truck that was our pride and joy. It was black with silver trim, with white wall tires, and it was NOT an automatic. The gears were on the column, making shifting easier with the crew on board. We had traded an old Buick sedan for the truck, along with a payment of five hundred dollars, our first bank loan. Somehow we all fit in the cab and back then car seats were not required. We must have passed the baby we all adored, back and forth a thousand times, for the interminable hours that we rode in search of a tree. The baby belonged to all of us, a sweet reminder of the sanctity of life.

When once our mission was complete, the *Varsity* in downtown Atlanta would be our destination - a chance to devour the greasy and spicy chili dogs for which they are famous. After hours of searching, we just could not seem to find the right Christmas tree; none of us were satisfied with what we had found. So, we exited the cab of that '64 pickup truck in the *Varsity* parking lot, unfurling our limbs, that had been compressed like an accordion and likewise, releasing harmonious sounds of pleasure that we had arrived! We launched ourselves into the sanctified grounds of *Varsity* heaven to engage in the long awaited meal that could send one's cholesterol level up a few notches in one sitting. We were oblivious to the hazards and too young to care.

After eating, it soon began to rain and we found ourselves riding home in the dark - treeless. Almost home, on the corner of the street, just above our apartment complex, we spotted trees for sale. Did we not see them when we began our mission that wonderful Sunday afternoon, full of excitement and anticipation? I suppose not. Yet then, after hours of searching the tree site was perfectly clear. In hindsight, we only saw the thrill of riding in that '64 Chevy, jammed in like sardines and having the time of our life, with precious cargo in our innocent care. The cold and crisp day that turned into an ugly rain did not deter us from the euphoric Christmas memory that still captures our hearts. Our perfect trees were just around the corner – our perfect day in a '64 Chevy pickup.

A Birthday to Remember
- or Forget

Great memories were made in that apartment. We were transformed from naive newlyweds into creatures of marital bliss. We worked and played, saved our money and took the plunge into parenthood, our ultimate goal to raise a family. Jess was born in that humble abode that was only about nine hundred square feet. He came into our life and we immediately knew the overwhelming joy that a child could bring. As a new mother, I learned quickly that he did not come with instructions. I tried to be the perfect mother and do everything right and was proud of my accomplishments with him. The months passed with a swiftness that hurled us toward a milestone that came all too soon - his first birthday.

Jess's big day came and we were excited to celebrate with a few friends and neighbors. I dressed him in the outfit that I had purchased especially for the celebration. His white high top shoes had been polished and shined - literally. I had carefully washed the strings, to a sparkling white, always striving for perfection. Shortly before the guests arrived, Jess began to cry. We had just finished eating a light supper and he had seemed fine.

The crying would not stop and we did everything to appease him. I tried everything, undressing him to make sure that the clothing was not at fault. At the suggestion of someone, I proceeded to give him a light enema. I was convinced that his stomach was hurting. Yes, I said enema, the evil word that makes even the brave cringe in trepidation. My precious little baby cried without ceasing, regardless of the gentle care I gave him as I administered the unpleasant task, all to no avail.

By this time, the guests were arriving and all waited patiently as we desperately struggled to soothe our son. We delayed the cutting of the cake and tried every trick in the book. Finally, we gave up and sat him in his high chair. His captive audience anxiously waited for the cake to be placed on his tray, symbolic of his first birthday. He sat there terribly unhappy and continued to cry. Any hope of witnessing him take the traditional dive into sugar heaven was fading fast. I knew I had to make a move.

As a last ditch effort, we removed Jess's shoes and socks.

My eyes caught sight of the tiny little toe that suddenly had a life of its own. Looking angry and red, it slowly sprang back to its rightful place, among its comrades. The source of all of the discomfort had been released from captivity and was finally free and without the help of an enema. The relief was immediate as Jess stopped crying and began to play. My anxiety vanished and my fears of having a socially inept child also.

Relief swept over me, as Jess attended the remainder of his birthday party shoeless and happy. I was devastated and embarrassed beyond words. I hid the tears that were silently flowing at intervals. I had failed him. Not only had I put his shoe on incorrectly, I had added the torment of an enema also. Actually, it was only a tiny bulb syringe that might have held a fourth cup of water. There was no damage to the toe, just my damaged pride.

What kind of mother would do such a thing? It was me, guilty as charged. I don't think he could have suffered as much physically as I did mentally for my mistake. The experience would serve me well in the future. I was summoned to the daycare center one day where Jess was attending. The caregiver could not seem to get him to stop crying. I calmly walked in and removed his shoes. There in one of the shoes was a toy soldier lying prone with his gun drawn and ready for action. The caregiver was stunned and slightly embarrassed. I was relieved and empowered by my knowledge.

The crinkled little toe was just an omen for the next few birthday celebrations, as Jess managed to pop his wrist out of joint a few days before he turned two. He broke his leg just above his ankle jumping off a step at the sitter's home just before turning four. I had quickly learned that boys will be boys and mothers will be human.

We lived in that apartment until Jess was two and a half and I was pregnant with our daughter, Katie. We had been patient and soon were blessed with a home. I still treasure some of the first recipes that were shared from those neighbors on the hill and will not discard the original handwritten copies.

Deborah's Chocolate Pie

One of my apartment neighbors would not allow her milk to waste, in fact, she did not waste anything. Routinely if her milk was running out of date, she found other ways to use it, most specifically in an old fashioned chocolate pie with meringue. That usually happened once a week and if lucky, I was the recipient of a piece of the delectable treat. I was not ashamed to accept a piece – anytime.

1 c. sugar
3 eggs
4 tbl. plain flour
2 c. milk
1 stick margarine or butter
2 tbl. cocoa
1 tsp. vanilla
Deep dish pie crust , prepared as directed on package.

Mix sugar, flour and cocoa well in a small mixing bowl. Separate the eggs, reserving the whites, and beat the yolks well by hand in a medium size mixing bowl. Add the milk and flavoring to the eggs and mix well. In the top of a double boiler, melt margarine. Whisk all of the ingredients into the melted margarine, continuously whisking, so that the eggs do not curdle. Cook in the top of the double boiler over medium high heat, stirring often, until very thick. Remove from heat and pour into the prepared pie crust.

Beat egg whites until they reach soft peaks and slowly add 3 tbl. of sugar and 1 tsp. vanilla, continuing to beat until stiff. Spoon egg whites over the chocolate mixture to form a meringue, using a fork to swirl peaks on top of the pie. Place in a 400 degree oven for 8 to 10 minutes, or until meringue is a golden brown. Allow pie to cool for at least two to three hours in the refrigerator before serving.

Denise's Blonde Brownies

This recipe that was shared over thirty five years ago brings back memories of another friend who lived in our apartment building, my friend Denise. That is the beauty in sharing a recipe. You may not see that person very often, but each and every time you prepare it, you will see them in your heart. My heart sees my friend making blonde brownies for her special occasions and my taste buds tingle at the thought of indulging in the chewy and flavorful morsels.

Preheat oven to 300 degrees.

1 lb. box of light brown sugar
3 eggs
1 stick margarine
2 c. self-rising flour
1 tsp. vanilla
1 c. chopped nuts

Cream butter and sugar with a mixer until smooth. Add eggs one at a time, beating until light and fluffy after each addition. Add flour and vanilla and beat until smooth. Stir in nuts. Spoon batter into a greased 9 X 13 inch baking dish. Bake at 300 degrees for 1 hour.

The Highway Life

It was a three bedroom, two bath brick ranch and it had the most amazing lawn and flower beds. Our first house was nine years old and as far as we were concerned, it was new. We dug our heels in and settled down into "our mansion" on Scenic Highway, which led and merged into the same Atlanta Highway in which I had lived as a child – full circle. The house was a dream that had come true, even though the interest rate was fifteen percent on our mortgage! It was the light at the end of the tunnel and the beginning of treasured outdoor space. The lawn itself was like a paradise, after living in the apartment for five years that did not even have a patio. Our apartment door had led to a breezeway that was shared with four other neighbors. Grilling out was not even an option. We were liberated!

Three weeks before the birth of our daughter, Katie, we moved our meager possessions into our first home. As mentioned before, we did not know the sex of our new daughter to be, savoring the days of anticipation of her birth. It was a glorious April day when she came into our world and we were blessed once again with a healthy baby.

We would return to our home some few days later to a full orchestration of the beauty of spring in all its glory. Our lawn encompassed a plethora of assorted plants, flowers and bushes. The seventy some odd azaleas that we could now call our own were in full bloom. The forsythia, commonly known as yellow belle, was aglow as radiant sunshine and all was right with the world. As I sat on the covered patio, looking down at Katie on one of those warm and magical days, I remember her in the tiny pink sun suit. There she was all pink and feminine and I knew that we would forever share womanhood. It was humbling, yet exhilarating.

I have always felt that the greatest gift that you could give a child is a brother or sister. We had accomplished that goal, but wanted to expand our family even more. In that endeavor, our little family grew to include another son, Josh. He was the caboose and boy did he make his mark. I knew he was my last and I spoiled him incessantly. My three children have been a source of great delight and overwhelming pride. I know they are not perfect, but they are my children, and that alone is enough for me. More than anything, they all value one another and love one another immensely. I wish that Katie could have had a sister and all of the wonderful joys that can come with that precious gift. Yet, she enjoys all of the attention that not one, but two brothers give her. Even though she will never experience the wonder of a sister, not in the sense that I have, I know she has created her own sisterhood with friends and more importantly for me, she is my lifelong friend.

I continued to try new recipes and even experimented with some canning in that Scenic Highway house. I rarely entertained, because we just could not afford it and eating out was a luxury. We were happy and lived modestly, fully aware that our family made us rich. We sacrificed everything for the needs of our children. We were not any different from anyone else. All of our friends did the same.

We lived on Scenic Highway for nine years and then we moved to what was then "the country." We bought an acre of land and built a home on it and there finished raising our children – on the piece of land that would be our haven. I named it God's Little Acre – I think there is a movie by that name. Deep in my heart, I wanted a place that my children could always call home, even when they were grown, one that they could always come back to visit. The two story white house with black shutters is that home.

Trailing Behind

Jan wed much later than I did, sixteen years to be exact. She was married in the same Methodist Church that I had been married. The stately church stood among the wonderful oak trees, one of its borders running beside the old parsonage where my grandmother had lived. The windows were and remain some of the most beautiful stained glass that I have ever seen, the grandeur of the structure, a fortress made of stone and mortar – a tribute to the strength of the Almighty Father. The stone porch was the same platform where our grandmother had once stood each Sunday after church, always there, always at church and always vocal.

Inside, the center aisle was covered with red carpet, flanked by the customary pews on either side, the familiar path to the altar – sacred. It was sacred to me beyond its own significance. The strains of *Oh Holy Night* sung by a beautiful girl that looked and sounded like an angel always rung in my ears when I entered the premises, someone I idolized who was much older. She never knew. The echoes of praise and the boisterous sound of my grandmother's voice – still there, beyond the quiet of the day I was home. It was Jan's day, but I was home.

During the wedding prayer, as I bowed my head, my sinuses began to release a slow drip that could not be stopped. As matron of honor, my hands were full of flowers and there was no way to wipe my nose. All that I could do was to sniff and sniff some more. Of course, everyone thought I was crying. No tears for me. I was elated that Jan was on the road to building her future and a family of her own, because I knew that was what she wanted most. We had orchestrated the wedding on a shoe string budget and it was lovely.

I had agreed to cater Jan's wedding reception. My ability to cook had risen to a new level and my confidence was high. I had expanded considerably my array of food choices to prepare. My chance to shine was within my grasp. The wedding reception would be small, between fifty and seventy five people. It would be in a comfortable setting and one that was an old friend to me, the First Methodist Church Social Hall.

Jan's friend helped me cater the wedding. Wedding

receptions had begun to include more than cake, nuts and punch, as it had been when I had married. The wedding fare of my time was simple and timeless, unlike the smorgasbords of today. We settled on a few light hor d'oeuvres.

The menu included stuffed and sliced chicken breasts, meatballs, tea biscuits, a fruit tray, and a vegetable tray. We also had punch, nuts, and of course a wedding cake. The meatballs were prepared from a recipe that I had acquired; none of those frozen ones from the wholesale chains for me. I thought that I had arrived when we served our guests!

My veggie dip was a hit, but not before it took a nosedive into the back of my SUV. I was able to salvage most of the dip, but the odor remained. When transporting food, you must have containers that are not only serviceable, but securely seal to protect the contents of your food. That odor stayed with the car. In fact, I never did get rid of the smell.

I had taken the first big step in preparing food for a large number of people and if success is measured in compliments – success was mine.

Jan was trailing behind as younger sisters do and the sixteen years I had experienced as wife and mother had put us in different places, but the gap was closing as she would eventually become a mother of four.

The recipes used for Jan's wedding were simple, but a challenge to prepare in large quantity. My favorite one has been a staple of many entertaining events over the years. I have adapted it to fit many occasions and have even changed the name when printing it on menus. It is the famous Vegetable Dip a.k.a Dill Spread.

Dill Spread

This recipe is one of the best vegetable dips I have ever tasted. It has a very unique flavor that compliments any raw vegetable with which you wish to serve.

1 c. sour cream
1 c. Hellman's® mayonnaise
1 small can of chopped black olives, drained well
2 tbl. dill weed, dried
2 tbl. onion flakes, dried
2 tbl. parsley, dried

Mix all ingredients in a food process, pulsing 3 to 4 times until well blended. Refrigerate overnight. Mix or shake well before using. Serve with raw vegetables.

*Additional dill can be added. It is also a great spread for toasted bread rounds. Top the bread rounds with dill dip and a thin slice of cucumber, for a great tea sandwich.

Shades of Childhood

Jan and I would find ourselves returning to the First Methodist Church a couple years later to witness the marriage of my father's only brother. His name was Julian Rupert. His first wife had died a few years before and loneliness led him to seek a second wife. He had no children. Julian was a well-known citizen and the former mayor of Loganville.

As I approached the church for the wedding ceremony, I observed a sign outside the church, proclaiming well wishes for Julian and his soon to be wife. It struck me as rather odd and I must say - something I had not witnessed before. I wondered if his previously elevated status of mayor warranted the signage. He was certainly one of the pillars of the Methodist Church. At my father's request, Jan and I would cut and serve the cake at the reception. She was there already seated and waiting for my arrival.

It was a cold day in February, but soon the church was filled with well-wishers, family and friends alike. For no apparent reason, Jan and I seemed to feel a bit giddy and laughter was just below the surface as we sat in the pews, waiting for the ceremony to begin. Maybe it was just the ghosts from our childhood taking over our spirits, forcing us to act as children sometimes do in Church – giggling. Jan and I sought to hide our laughter and remain ladies with our manners intact. We certainly would not tarnish our reputations as being rude. The wedding party entered and we became respectful and reverent.

Just when we thought that we had our emotions under control, from the side door, and in front of the congregation, there appeared my Great Uncle Hines, who was at least ninety five at the time. He had arrived via the assisted living facility that he called home and there draped on his arm was a woman. She was about twenty years his junior and could have passed as a double for Bette Davis! An obvious wig was on her head, adorned with a red tam that sat nilly-willy on the side of her head. Her lips were of the brightest red and her eyelashes could not deceive us of their origin – fake! Hines was bent over and seemed to be taking the lead, even in his ninety plus years. His entrance was so profound that any hopes

129

of our gaining a serious composure was far beyond my expectation. I dropped my head as the soloist began her high pitched song and tried to suppress the laughter that was causing me to tremble. I cut my eyes over to Jan and she was replicating my demeanor. The chosen song and music, sung in a high pitch, only served to increase our mirth, but soon it was over. We both raised our heads, not daring to look at one another, even to spare a quick look to measure the other's composure. Becoming lost in the moment and reverting back to our childhood days - in our comfort zone - as little children forgetting just where we were. Soon the childhood ghosts were exorcised from our bodies. There we sat as staunch as anyone could ask of a lady, heads held high and none the wiser of our temporary loss of wits.

Cooking with Class

Raising three children can be a challenge and so expensive. After my husband had an unexpected career change, I decided to begin a part-time venture – cooking instruction in my home. I did this in addition to working full time, arranging the sessions somewhat like the hostess parties of which most of us are familiar.

Advertising through my friends was easy and I emphasized cooking classes as the perfect venue for a birthday party. I organized several of those and they were a great success.

My primary idea was to teach young ladies to cook. I thought it was a great concept, because I had already discovered that most women my age had no cooking skills, much less to offer instruction to their own children. I gave a few lessons to some young ladies, but the word got out at my place of employment and soon the twenty-somethings were at my door.

It was easy enough for me to teach the classes. The most valuable skill that my mother had taught me was how to prepare a meal in a timely manner and complete all of the menu items to serve simultaneously. I would first shop for my ingredients the evening before. The cooking tools would be arranged on the counter and the ingredients would be organized for each menu item that I would demonstrate.

The guests got a lot of bang for their buck. When they arrived, I had hor d'oeuvres prepared, usually hot and right out of the oven. As they devoured the treat, I would give them a demonstration of how it was made. The dessert was demonstrated next, so that if cooking time was needed or refrigeration was required, it would be ready to eat at the end of our session. The main course would usually be a meat, accompanied by two vegetables and a selection of homemade bread. All of this was done beginning at six o'clock p.m. I got off at five o'clock and drove the fifteen minutes it took to reach my home. I prepared the hor d'oeuvres and it was ready to serve by the time the students arrived.

It took about an hour and a half to demonstrate all of the menu items. Not only did the students receive instruction, they were asked to participate in the preparation. They were then seated in my dining room and were served the meal, while I cleaned the kitchen. All for twenty dollars per person! I felt guilty for charging so much, not realizing what a deal they were getting. I gave them the recipes and they gave me a chance to gain more confidence in my cooking abilities.

It was a great experience and it was easy enough to cook for six, the number I chose to instruct, since I had learned to cook for that number, while growing up. Some of those students still relate their enjoyment of the classes to me and their continued use of the recipes that I shared. It was my instruction, but I was ever the student, learning from those who were oblivious that they were in fact teaching me.

One of my favorite appetizers was simple to prepare and smelled "oh so heavenly". When the eager participants arrived, they welcomed the smell of the bacon used and were surprised at the additional ingredients.

Bacon Wrapped Wafers

Preheat oven to 300 degrees.

1 box of club crackers
1 8 oz. container of cream cheese, softened
1 lb. of very lean bacon, vertically sliced in half

Purchase club crackers that are packaged as singles. Spread about 1 ½ tbl. of cream cheese on a wafer as you would peanut butter. Place another wafer on top to form a sandwich. Center wafer on one of the half slices of bacon cross-wise. Fold bacon to center from both directions, overlapping on one side. Repeat with remaining wafers, until the quantity you desire. Place wafers seam side down on an oven broiler pan (this will allow bacon grease to drip down). Bake 20 to 25 minutes on 300 degrees till golden brown.

Catering Ventures

My cooking school idea seemed to vanish beneath my eyes as I was hired for my first paid catering job. It was a chance for me to increase my income on a greater level without putting forth any more effort than the cooking classes required. Janet, owner of the company that I worked for at the time, asked me to cater a baby shower luncheon for one of the employees of the company. I was flattered and eager to do my best. Apparently, I was a great success, as I found myself catering for many more events to come.

Janet, who has become a dear friend, is one of the most gracious women that I have ever met. Savannah born and bred, she is the epitome of graciousness and a product of the genteel heritage of which Savannah is known. Many of my catering jobs were held in her beautiful home in which she has shared with both friends and family as a generous hostess. I quickly became acclimated to her kitchen and dining area, a treasure chest of lovely serving pieces, china and stemware. It was a great and wonderful experience to prepare and serve her guests. Her guests were mine!

The satisfaction that I gained could not be measured in the monetary compensation that I received. I cooked and served the dishes in much of my own antique glassware that I had begun to collect. Janet's array of serving pieces and dishes were there at my disposal, but I know that she sensed my pride in sharing my treasures. It was such a pleasure to be a part of entertaining others in such a gracious manner. You might say I lived vicariously through my catering in her beautiful home. I was always presented to the guests as a viable part of the party's success and the praises were not left on deaf ears. I could not have been any more pleased if I had been the hostess myself. I gave all of my catering jobs the care that I would use for my own family or friends. How could I do anything less?

Code of Honor

I had catered Jan's wedding and felt confident that I could do it again. My first opportunity to cater a wedding and get paid came, but the chance to make a reasonable profit was lost in my inability to charge enough for the affair. It was a great experience and one in which I remember well. The event facility was in the old Women's Female Seminary in Lawrenceville. It was quaint and held the charm of any historical venue. The wedding was held outside, and when the one hundred guests made their way to the buffet, I was ready. The bride had chosen a "mini meal" to offer her guests, since it was a mid-day wedding. A "mini meal" consists of the same offerings of a dinner selection, but in smaller quantities that included some hor d'oeuvres.

One of the special dishes that I prepared was green bean bundles. I stood behind the buffet and served the guests as they came through the line, giving them a verbal description of the foods that I had prepared. One very hungry and abrasive guest, started to eat from her plate in the serving line. As she began to devour the green bean bundles from her plate, her exclamations of praise were hard to ignore. She then began to quiz me for the ingredients used in the bundles, while standing in the line. I was not able to give her the answer she was waiting to hear, as it was obvious that I was fully occupied with the other guests.

I slipped back into the kitchen behind the buffet in an effort to refill one of the trays. The tiny kitchen was just that – tiny! It was insufficient in its offering of workspace required for the food preparation. I felt tense and apprehensive as I replenished the tray with my selections. It was stressful to be in such a confined work space.

After completing my mission, I proceeded to exit the kitchen, tray in hand. I opened the door to enter the room. There I met her, face to face. She was a few inches taller than me and she stared right into my eyes with all the determination that she could muster. She said to me, "You are going to give me that recipe, aren't you?" I was so taken aback and stunned, not believing that I had just opened the door to this ill-mannered guest, who deserved no more than my look of sheer disbelief. I quickly regained my composure and said

134

with all of the genteel sweetness that I could maintain without revealing my true feelings, "I am sorry, I don't share my recipes." She was shocked and could not find any words of rebuttal, as I continued on my mission to replenish the buffet. She was so insulted by my reply that she reported my "rudeness" to the mother of the bride, who found it rather amusing that the guest was somewhat confused in her assessment of the situation.

Recipes are priceless and sometimes coveted by those who wish to replicate them and serve at every social event that is held with a meal attached. I did not want green bean bundles to be a staple at every church social in Gwinnett County. Neither did I wish for the abrasive and pushy woman to take one ounce of credit in her own arena for my green bean bundles. There is a code of honor among us who recognize the care and pride of cooking for pleasure, we do share. Somehow she did not fit the mold. The recipe has remained undisclosed and at my discretion, will be revealed on one of the following pages as my catering business has now culminated into a fond memory. The recipe did not belong to me personally, it was not my possession, but as a caterer, I chose not to share it at the time.

The years I spent catering were rewarding. I gave it my all and only had a few regular customers, all that I could handle. Yet, I was willing to take on some very interesting jobs. I prepared food for small dinner parties, office parties, showers, bridal luncheons and even a Thanksgiving dinner. There were only three occasions in which I catered a wedding reception for someone other than a family member, just too risky - someone's big day. The details are endless and the stress unending.

A Dose of Humility

In a weak moment, I contracted with one other person to cater a wedding reception. I found myself in a multi-million dollar home in the suburbs of Atlanta, planning the reception. The bride wanted a mini-meal. She was young and unpretentious. The older man that she was going to marry left the arrangements to her discretion. As a few months passed, it was evident that the ceremony would be delayed until the next year. It was a wedding that did not happen and I not sure that it ever did. She had presented me with a down payment, enough to cover the cost of the food. I agreed that she could use her down payment toward the cost of a Christmas party.

The receiving area for the party was much like the lobby of a hotel. The home was large and cold, no warmth to be found, much like the guests that attended the affair. I found myself in the midst of some very pretentious guests. I had just stepped into the dining area with one of my beautiful milk glass pedestal compotes. It had lattice work around its white edge, interwoven with jeweled red berries that I had added for color. The red against the white was certainly dramatic, simple and quite beautiful for the season. My thoughts were interrupted when a very beautifully dressed and bejeweled female exclaimed, "That is lovely. Where did you find it?" I was quick to reply in my soft southern drawl, "Oh, I just can't remember where I purchased it".

As I turned my back and walked to the kitchen, I suppressed a smile as I wondered what she would have thought of learning the truth. I could have replied, "My mother purchased it at a yard sale for fifty cents!" I was not ashamed of where I had acquired the compote, but I was not sure that her constitution could handle the news. The compote is one of my most treasured pieces of glass and I continue to use it every Christmas with those same red berries, a reminder of humility.

Glassware Speaks

My love for cooking has a strong parallel to serving pieces. Imagining a beautiful piece of china, filled with a delectable dish will always capture my interest. My addiction to glassware began even before I realized that I was addicted. My mother was the influence and in the beginning I was not a willing partner. She began collecting Depression glass and just beautiful cut glass in general, during the early years of my marriage. She would spend hours in the thrift and antique shops plundering, searching for a treasure.

136

When I would visit, she would carefully remove her new found treasure from old newspaper. It would reveal a piece of glass and then, nonchalantly I would praise her find, secretly not that impressed. As time moved on and I started to appreciate the beauty of the sparkling treasure, I began to get the fever. The pieces that were designed back in the forties are so unusual.

My addiction turned into a collection of at least ten antique punch bowls, from small to very large. Some of the bowls look like diamonds that have been cut and their value is only equal to the love and care that I give them. They are rich in heritage and a reminder that they were once loved by someone who was must have been equally as proud.

Sometimes, I visualize a lovely dish brimming to the rim with food, and immediately start planning a party or a meal that will include using the dish. I still enjoy my attempts to capture the past and admit that I will exercise my right to those passionate thoughts. After all, we must all have at least one vice.

After many years of catering on a small scale and never choosing to create large quantities, and in my estimation, sacrificing quality, I surrendered my apron. I went quietly, but sure that I had made an impact for those I prepared food and served, today, steadfast in my belief that I was a success.

A Glimpse Can Last a Lifetime

As life would have it, my children went away to college before I could blink an eye. The children were gone and so was I. Somehow, I had lost myself along the way. I knew that I had to find the woman that was lost deep inside. That is what happens when women trade themselves for motherhood, somehow forgetting that they really exist. Guilty and not ashamed – it was worth the ride, and the ground felt good when I touched it after twenty five years.

There was just never enough time to explore the possibilities at hand when it came to decorating, cooking and entertaining. I was too busy being a mother. At last, I could follow the desires of my heart. I had never had time to entertain my friends and family, on the scale that I so desired, preparing food and using all of the treasured items that I had collected for the past years. I wanted to use my linen, china, crystal and silver, and for those items to be appreciated. I dreamed of creating table settings that would be remembered always by my guests and as a tribute to my affection for them.

Tea parties were the rage and my answer. The idea to host the parties came at Christmas a few years ago. Of course it is a time when we are all too rushed to think of anything, but getting through the season. I began that first year, by ignoring the gift buying frenzy. I refused to allow it to be a priority. I gave about nine parties in the three weeks before Christmas. They were not large affairs. Most of the parties were for only a few guests, an opportunity for me to make them all feel special. It was my gift to them and to me, because my pleasure was immense. Some of those friends, I never see, but on occasion, maybe once or twice a year. Some of them I may not see for years. I hope they remember our special moments of friendship. I will cherish them always, just as a cup of hot tea.

Over the years, I have learned that some friends come and go and the circumstances are many times beyond our control. Yet, each and every friendship helps to shape us all. As we grow in our busy lives, our families grow and our focus changes. That is why, it is important to enjoy the time at hand with the friends that God has given us. He places each and every person in our lives for a purpose, maybe for them, to see a glimpse of who we are and for us to make a lasting impression. Whether they are there for a moment or there for the duration, the impact is ours to make – a glimpse of true friendship can last a lifetime.

Savories and beverages used for these intimate events came from some of my cookbooks especially written for tea parties. One of my favorite recipes was shared from a friend when I attended a birthday party at Christmas.

Wassail

Not only does this drink taste wonderful, it will smell heavenly, especially during the holidays.

½ gallon apple cider
1 ½ quart cranberry juice cocktail
¼ c. brown sugar
4 sticks cinnamon
2 tsp. cloves

Combine ingredients in a 4 qt. stockpot. Bring to a boil over medium high heat. Reduce heat and simmer for 20 minutes, then remove cloves. Serve warm.

The Butterfly Has Metamorphosed

Most young girls dream of a wedding someday and I would suffice it to say that most mothers share that dream as well. It is certainly something that I looked forward to and since I only had one daughter, I wanted her wedding to be perfect. Having said that, I found myself transitioning into another phase of my life; another generation would begin with the marriage of my daughter.

When Katie announced her engagement, it was the beginning of the dream wedding that I had always hoped that her father and I could provide for her and her future husband. It was my opportunity to entertain our family and friends at her reception on a level, as I had never done before. I wanted to show them our appreciation for being a part of our lives, as our children grew and matured into adults. After all, they also had helped to shape our children's lives. Weddings and births are a celebration held in highest esteem in my measure. We wanted to include each and every friend and family member that had been a part of our child's life, if at all possible and within reason. It was a chance for those who we loved and who loved us to share in God's plan as it had come full circle.

As most of us Southern women do, I had been planning for years, some might say since birth, for Katie's special day. Fortunately, for the both of us, she and I only had a couple of disagreements in the planning stage. She was totally on board with everything that I suggested. I almost became perturbed with her complacency, loving to plan, but craving her participation.

Katie put her trust in me because she knew I lived and breathed to create and decorate, and rarely did she disapprove of my choices. Well, maybe the dresses which still hang in a closet upstairs. They were purchased for a children's tea party, but I thought I could transform them into "fairy dresses" and they would be great for the wedding. What's wrong with a few fairies floating around the reception to give out the favors? And wasn't that beautiful arch of flowers I had seen in a magazine to be held by the flower girls really unique? The question was what to do with the arch of flowers during the ceremony, when two little girls' arms give out? It might have gotten a little hard to hold up. Okay, so I got a

140

little carried away. Magazines are dreamy, but reality set in.

I would have loved to have hosted the wedding reception at my home, complete with tents and a band. We definitely had the room for it and parking could be arranged. Our acre lot in the country was the perfect place. There is something about the home that makes celebrations so personal, but I knew in my heart the idea was not a practical one.

The idea of family and friends to put together a reception was so attractive to me and there was a group of us who had already done so with their daughters. I wanted a *Steel Magnolias* wedding for Katie, just like in the movie, one where friends are an integral part of the day. I certainly could not get Katie off of Cloud Nine to be of any assistance. Some people spend thousands to achieve a beautiful memory, but lose the magic of the village. I truly believe in the African proverb, "It takes a village to raise a child." With the help of my friends, my village became a reality.

For me, as a mother, my daughter's wedding was the finale of a beautiful woman setting sail on her own journey to complete her passage into womanhood, equipped with all the love and support of her family. Most importantly, equipped to be kind and considerate, caring and loving, a reflection of all of the qualities in which had I tried so hard to instill. As she was always told, "It is more important to be beautiful on the inside". I still see that in her today just as I did then, and I hope others do as well.

Katie and I agreed on the venue that both of us loved. It was the historical courthouse in Gwinnett County. As a history buff, I was thrilled. Katie had her heart set on it and we could not have chosen any better. It was only four miles from our home and that in itself was a blessing.

My search for a caterer had begun early on in the planning process. In a weak moment, I let a friend talk me in to catering the wedding reception. I had recently orchestrated a reception for her daughter and knew it could be accomplished. There was only one hitch. The venue did not have a full kitchen and the organization of the final preparation of hot food would be a challenge. So in a moment of delirium and insanity, I decided to cater my own daughter's wedding, of course, with plenty of help from friends. I was challenged by a friend who could not believe my decision. Her remark to me was, "I just don't want to see you looking tired and stressed at the reception." It was a test and I was out to prove that I could play the part of the relaxed mother of the bride. Okay, I could never be relaxed, but I was determined to meet the challenge graciously.

The details on the decorations and theme for the reception would have been enough for me to undertake, much less preparing and coordinating the food. I just didn't know where to stop when planning the decorations. As I said before, I think all women dream of their daughter's wedding from the time they are born. Was it a mistake to orchestrate and cater my own daughter's wedding? Yes and no, I would probably do it all again, but I don't know how I kept my sanity.

The venue housed a beautiful old courtroom that included tables and chairs for seating of guests. Linens, table arrangements and any other item that a demented soul, such as I could dream up, would have to be acquired, transported, arranged and then disassembled in a seven hour time span. I even paid for more time, just to decorate the venue, but we could not begin decorating until ten in the morning on the day of the wedding. I would be an integral part of the ceremony; after all, I was the mother of the bride.

The wedding ceremony was at five which only gave me a few hours to assist with finalizing the decorations - just a tiny detail, in the grand scheme of things. Let's add coordination of the food preparation on that day to send a person to the nut house. It was just the distraction I needed, because as happy as I was, I needed that distraction. I love hard and I love deep, it was going to be hard to say goodbye.

As I have planned and orchestrated many parties, luncheons and showers over the years, I have learned a few tricks of the trade. Think Christmas. The decorations really offer some great options for décor that can be used all year round. In fact, I had been buying pink decorations for several years, because I had known that Katie wanted a wedding with a pink theme. There are some wonderful items that are so reasonable that can be used for table decorations or anything your imagination will allow. That is how our butterfly theme evolved. It is amazing how the eye can see things that normally would just go unnoticed, if you are planning an event, no matter the occasion. Katie was ecstatic with our plans.

While out shopping for the wedding, suddenly, everything

pink caught my eye, and it was hard not to go beyond the limit with purchases. I like the rule, less is more, and no overkill. I tried to keep that in mind and hope that pink and silver butterflies, will be remembered as lovely and magical by friends and family for they were in abundance. Most importantly, remembered by Katie as she experienced one of the most important days of her life.

The menu was planned and agreed upon by Katie as soon as the decision was made for me to cater the wedding. If it weren't for my family and friends, I couldn't and wouldn't write about the most beautiful wedding and reception I had ever seen, at least in my eyes. My wonderful friends made it possible. Warning! Please do not try to duplicate anything that I did without some very reliable friends and in my case, some very good hired assistants.

In my search for hired assistants, I hired someone who had experience in catering, and who could supervise serving of the food - someone who could replace me, since I had to step aside on the day of the wedding. I hired a lady who I had only just met a few times. She was older and had quite a few years of catering experience under her belt, and I was sure she fit the bill. All of the food would be prepared by me and my friends in the preceding days before the wedding day. She would supervise the buffet stations and be responsible for their replenishment, in addition to arriving early to assist in the final details. We had three different planning sessions that lasted all day to discuss and prepare her for all that was expected on the day of the wedding. I also made dinner and had a planning session with my friends to discuss everyone's role.

I chose the perfect hostess in my friend Patti, who is as southern as they come. I hired a gentleman whose expertise was in cooking meat and he was in charge of the carving station. His assistant had a nickname of "Peaches". He was rather debonair in his chef's hat and fit the bill quite nicely. In fact, several of the people who were hired had colorful names. The lady who prepared the grits and who did a splendid job had a name that was pronounced, "Kook". Two additional ladies were hired for the kitchen coordination where their expertise could be used best. The mushroom fondue, creamed spinach and without a question, those green bean bundles held in high esteem by an unknown guest at another wedding reception were to be among some of the day's offerings. I would be at the mercy of those assistants and God's too, as I soon found out.

After months of planning, the finale began. Food preparations began on Thursday, green beans bundles were made by the hundreds, all with the help of my friends. Sauces and spreads were prepared earlier in the week, and the side dishes were completed as well. Arrangements were made for the use of the commercial ovens at the church where the wedding would take place, then transported to the venue, shortly before the reception would begin. It was a little less than a mile from the church to the historic courthouse. Carefully coordinated with friends and those hired to supervise, the plans were in place and all of the players had their roles. There were fifteen people who would assist in the decorating of the venue, and to set up the buffet for the wedding.

The morning of the wedding, I found myself on the screened porch, cutting roses for the guest tables at the reception. There was no time to think, to feel - to realize what that day would essentially bring – the end to a lifelong dream. I suppose that deep in the recesses of my mind, I deliberately planned it that way. I was too busy to allow the depth of emotion to put a chokehold on my heart; otherwise I think I would have forgotten to breathe. There was so much detail and my friends would soon be at the venue to begin the decoration process and I was scheduled to join them by noon.

The bridesmaids arrived at eleven to gather for pictures to be made outside my neighbor's pool and lush gardens. Their gardens were a reflection of their expertise in horticulture and I knew the backdrop for pictures would be magnificent.

Before I knew it, I was in route to the courthouse to assist with the decorations. My wonderful group of friends had been there for two hours prior to my arrival. Unfortunately, since it was a public venue, the rental window allowed very little time for preparation in advance of the reception. There was no access for preparations prior to the wedding day, other than to deliver the decorations to a locked room. Rented linens for tables and chairs were already in place. All of my many, many serving pieces that I had carefully chosen had been delivered the day before also. Each and every one of them held the fondness of a sentimental woman with a penchant for the past. Many of the pieces were purchased from proceeds of my catering days.

There could not have been enough hours in a day, much less

the seven allocated before the reception, that would have been enough for me to decorate. I knew that I must use the precious two hours I had to spend, before my scheduled arrival at the church, very wisely. All of my friends were there for me, to fulfill the great and mighty tall order before them. Even though I could only participate in decorating for the two hours, I knew that my plans were unshakeable. I had simply worked too hard, planned too much and even had even prepared a document outlining the details of the placement of each and every decoration, serving piece and buffet set-up. Then the shock of my life came.

I thought I had made it! After months of planning, the one star that I thought I had chosen well would let me down. Why didn't I see that she was just not up to the task? The lady I hired was in her early sixties and had owned a bridal shop, and as I said earlier, had catered for years in the past. Had I not spent hours with her going over all of the details to supervise and make everything happen, just as if I were there to do it myself?

After arriving over an hour late, this "well chosen" lady looked at me five hours before the reception and said, "This is not what I had expected". It was about thirty minutes before I was to leave for the church to meet the photographer for the final pictures prior to the ceremony. We were in that tiny kitchen that had been my one reservation in renting the venue. The walls started to close in around me. Memories of another tiny kitchen and another lady came to my mind, but this time, I was about to lose control. None of the confidence I had felt in that other kitchen could surface to strengthen my reserve to respond appropriately to her statement.

I was so shocked, I walked over to the refrigerator and opened the door, not really knowing what I was doing – trance like. My palms were sweating and my heart had skipped a beat. My mouth was so dry, that it was hard to swallow. I started to shake as I reached for the "dill spread" and in slow motion; I saw it drop to the floor. It hit my shoe with a splash, the dip slowly creeping down the bottom of my dress, like a paint brush that had been over filled. "It's just your work clothes," I told myself as I stood there immobilized.

Images of the spilled dip at my sister's wedding flashed before my eyes. It seemed that the smell had never left my nostrils and I momentarily stopped breathing. The startling realization came

145

that this was not just any wedding reception, it was my daughter's – what had I done? In my trancelike state, I walked to the sink, pulled up the bottom of my dress, turned on the water and began to wash my dress. As I squeezed the water out of the dress, I thought I would lose my composure, but it was already gone. Slowly, I came back to reality as my friend Sheri repeated again, "Renee, just tell us what you want us to do." Her words penetrated my temporary loss of senses. I snapped back to reality when I heard those words, knowing in that moment, that the storm was over and we would prevail – by sheer will alone, my friends became my army. I was armed with absolute determination from head to toe as a sense of peace surrounded me. We would be the champions of this unexpected turn of events. My friend Brenda joined in with all the others to do what good friends do best – to be there for you. I left for the church, prayed for peace and knew that not only was I at the mercy of my chosen army, I was at God's mercy as well. I was at peace.

I would arrive at the church to find my daughter completing her final touches that would make her, to me, the most beautiful bride I had ever seen. Thank goodness, modern protocol allowed for the pink wedding that Katie had dreamed of to become acceptable for the fall of the year. Butterflies became magical in shades of pink and silver on that day. The bridesmaids wore strapless mossy green dresses, with sashes that fell from dreamy bows tied in the back, softly flowing to create a feminine bustle. The junior bridesmaid wore white, trimmed in a pink sash. The bottom of the skirt danced with pink flowers with green leaves. Tiny flowers girls wore white duponi silk, jeweled necklines and puffed sleeves, trimmed with a pink sash to match the junior bridesmaid.

Members of the wedding party found themselves in the church sanctuary to have photos made before the ceremony. It was the first time that anyone had seen my dress, as I wanted it to be a surprise to my family. Mary Frances complimented my dress by saying, "You look so beautiful in that dress". I was so pleased, but as usual, I could not fully accept a compliment. I replied, "Thank you, I worked very hard to get rid of my fat rolls". Then came her very blunt in her reply, "Well, you still have some. I saw them last night at the rehearsal dinner!" Touché´. Suffice it to say, I did not reply.

146

The ceremony was beautiful, a harpist played a Scottish ballad as the mothers were seated, a tribute to the Scottish heritage of our new son-in-law. Katie was in white, strapless chiffon, with a full skirt, tucked and tied into clouds that billowed in strategic places, with a long train adorned in silver beadwork. The silver jeweled bodice and train sparked like diamonds as she floated down the aisle. I smiled a gentle nudge into her eyes, as she looked as though she might cry. My face mimicked her same expression, but I remained steadfast in my resolve, swallowing my own tears away.

It was a beautiful ceremony, a tribute to their love for the Lord. The Lord's Prayer was sung, bride and groom were married and I did not shed a tear, but a river would have flowed, had I allowed the floodgates to open. I could not keep my mind off of the reception and I was glad for the diversion. The hopeless romantic in me would have cried tears of joy, yet feelings of sadness were running rampant through my heart. Mascara would have made a roadmap down my face and how could I turn to greet the guests? Instead, I focused on the reception, trying hard not to acknowledge the finality of my role as it had been since Katie's birth. She was married in just a few short minutes of orchestrated bliss in the sight of God and in his house.

The magical day continued when the horse drawn carriage arrived, complete with a bearded driver, looking as though he came right from a movie set. He had a long beard and wore a top hat. The little flower girls gasped, saying, "Look, its beauty and the beast!" The bride and groom were whisked away for the short ride to the courthouse. They made their way around the downtown square to prolong their journey and to relish the moments of a newly married couple. Guests were waiting on the historical courthouse lawn as the carriage arrived with the bride and groom. The newlyweds departed the carriage and welcomed their guests by releasing beautiful monarch butterflies from a white hat box tied with a satin ribbon. I was on auto pilot by then, anxious to enter the reception, as soon as possible.

The couple quickly ascended the stairs up to the second floor ballroom. There was a balcony at this historical site used in the early days for dignitaries to speak to the audience below. It remained closed for visitors, but on this day, Katie would toss her bouquet from the balcony, as the young ladies gathered for a chance to catch the treasure. She stood there regally as if she were to give a formal speech, smiling above the tulle that secured wreaths of pink and green.

Katie turned and tossed the bouquet through the air and it soared as if it had wings. A flash of gray caught my eye as I saw someone lunging for the bouquet and then it landed in the outstretched arms of an undisclosed family member – suffice it to say, her age of seventy four years sent waves of shock through the disbelieving crowd. She proudly held it up, oblivious to the audience and their disbelief. The audience grew silent and the question on everyone's mind was, "Who was that?"

I barely realized what had happened and moved toward the stairs, not believing what I had just seen. Recollections of the outrageous character "Weezer" in the movie *Steel Magnolias* were racing back to my mind. Could it be that she was in our presence? Maybe the culprit had suffered a moment of insanity or had she just reverted back to her younger self? The moment was lost forever and Katie moved on to the enchantment of the day. Forgiven, but not forgotten.

I can't tell you the feeling that I had, when I began my journey up the courthouse stairs that led to the second level of the building. When I had envisioned the staircases, I knew I had wanted to make a statement as guests ascended the stairs for the reception room. In my eyes, that statement was bold and beautiful, far exceeding what I had planned. The stately building offering its proud staircases of dark rich wood and carved spindles for guests to ascend, today were bearing tulle of pink and white, adorned in magical pink and silver. The banisters were draped with more of the pink and white tulle, caught at intervals with cones filled with white roses. Jeweled butterflies were scattered throughout.

When I looked into the ballroom, I saw tables bathed in white cloths, with centerpieces of silver trays. In the center of the trays, a silver goblet held white roses with touches of pink and silver, a glittering butterfly strategically placed amongst the roses. Beaded hearts lay on the trays, a tribute to the significance of the day. The chairs had white covers with silver and pink bows tied alternately, around the backs of the chairs. Each chair had a pink or silver symbol of love tied in the center of the bow. Printed menus were framed with lacy cutwork edging, and embossed with a silver butterfly, placed on white paper doilies that marked each place setting.

The large windows in the reception area, which had once been a court room, had magnificent arched windows with wide window sills. They held pink and white potted pansies in silver wrappers, waiting for guests to take them home as a token of appreciation. Pink butterfly candles danced above them in glass pedestal containers. I was in awe of how it had all come together, since I had left the venue before the final touches were complete. The effect was more than I could have ever anticipated.

A special table had been set for the bride and groom in the center of the room mirroring the same pinks and silvers surrounding it, but set with china uniquely chosen for the bridal couple. The bridal party table had a centerpiece that consisted of stacked glass trays, tiered as tall as a wedding cake, with tiny petit fours filling each tray. On either side of the centerpiece, flowers arranged in antique cherub containers were both beautiful and sentimental. One of them had three angels of porcelain, holding the flowers in an urn above their heads – a reminder of my three children that God had given me. I had made a pledge to myself to use it when Katie married. It was one of the first antique pieces that I had bought with money from my first catering job. The other urn, I had found earlier that summer. The single angel as the base of the vessel, again holding an urn was a reminder of my new son, who until now had no siblings.

The courtroom had come alive and now was the site of months of planning and the reality of it all was incomprehensible. The buffet table was just as inviting as I imagined it would be in its every detail. The t-shaped configuration held the silk arrangement I had made in the center of its juncture. It had pinks and greens and long weeping stems that held sparkling clear stones. It was regal in its silver urn and had been a work of love, when I created it just for the day.

As I spied the carving station, I saw a big guy with a great smile, and he looked the perfect chef, as he carved his delicious beef filet and Applewood smoked pork tenderloin. He had great successes in his cook-off endeavors in the barbeque arena, and we were lucky to have his expertise. A chef from the finest restaurant could not have done a better job.

A shrimp and grits bar was stationed on the other side of the room. Clear goblets were stacked in a beautiful display, inviting guests to fill one with the grits and shrimp sauce. I had found a beautiful mermaid statue that was placed high above the table. Cut pink sea shells were fashioned into use as napkin rings.

I had been most concerned about the success of the shrimp and grits bar. That success depended on all of the cards falling into place. The sauce made for the shrimp, had to be added at the last few minutes. The grits were delivered at the last hour before the reception began. They were in a cooler which actually will maintain heat for an extended length of time. The grits stayed piping hot in that vessel and were delicious. Those plans went off without a hitch and I had rave reviews. The recipe was my own and its debut was well received. The goblets made it fun and they were a hit as an appetizer to begin the evening. Some even chose the shrimp and grits as their meal.

Those shrimp and grits have become a source of unending needling from my son-in-law, who loves to eat and counted the days for the wedding feast. The couple was served first and I was anxious for them to have their first dance. I thought they had ample time to eat and I kept prodding the disc jockey to announce the dance. What I didn't observe was the constant interruptions that kept them from consuming their food. I will never live that down, but I have made amends. I have repeated the feast on more than one occasion, of course not in its entirety. He will have a lifetime of shrimp and grits, but I will never hear the end of that story.

I blinked and the day was gone forever, with nothing left, but the remnants of all of the endeavors of my labor and the hard work of my friends. The clean-up was tedious, yet swift in relation to all the hours spent placing decorations and the months of their preparation. All of us moved through the clean-up process like programmed robots. We had a deadline to vacate the premises and it was met on time, slightly before twelve a.m. Just like Cinderella, we dashed to our vehicles at the stroke of midnight, with pink and silver butterflies, now stored in boxes, carrying flowers that now bowed their heads as their life was beginning to wane. They had served their noble purpose and so had we. We had given our daughter the wedding of her dreams. Rest did not come easy in those early hours when we reached our home, as my eyes closed to find pink and silver butterflies fluttering in my mind, their wings finally finding their resting place as exhaustion overtook my mind and soul.

And then there were the heels, tall black spikes, Katie's trademark-silently lying by the door at home. They seemed lonely without their owner, lost without those tiny feet that occupied them, elevating the five foot one inch girl to a height that made her feel taller and more confident. I spotted them that next morning as I drug my tired and exhausted body from room to room, totally lost as what to do next, not knowing how to think without a wedding to plan. I suddenly walked into the dining room. There it was - the portrait that we had made a few weeks before and displayed at the wedding. I reached out and touched her face, admiring every detail of her sitting there in the beautiful green grass - the backdrop of God's creation. She was in a cloud of white, the only thing missing, I thought was a pair of wings, after all, she was my angel – my only daughter. The tears came and all of the emotions that were pent up inside overflowed, motherhood at its best - my finest hour – a beginning and an end. Suddenly those black spike heels and their many companions that I sometimes found myself tripping over became a rite of passage. The shoes that she had discarded, now the only remnants of her presence signified that she was gone from our home forever. The butterfly had metamorphosed and I was elated and proud.

Thirteen Months: Two Weddings

Another love story began on that October wedding day and would culminate just a short thirteen months later, as my older son Jess began dating Heather, one of the bridesmaids. She had been Katie's college roommate and sparks flew into a whirlwind romance. Admittedly, the two of them had previously been attracted to one another, but timing was everything. It was now their time and soon mine to start planning. My swansong in the catering arena was still raw and emotional. What better way to cure those feelings, than to start planning a rehearsal dinner for their wedding?

So, without further ado, I began planning Jess and Heather's rehearsal dinner, but this time I had it catered. The preparation for

151

the dinner party and decorations were enough to keep me occupied for some months. I had finally allowed myself to let go of the concept of doing it all. There was a wonderful Cajun restaurant that specialized in fresh seafood that we hired, and it felt good. I could fully focus on decorating the venue for the rehearsal dinner.

The wedding was in the fall of the year. The colors were champagne and red and visions of tiny white pumpkins and glossy red apples were filling my head, threatening to overtake any normal thoughts required to function on a daily basis.

We secured a venue in the small town of Fayetteville, Georgia; the old train depot had been restored and was available for rent. It was a bare bones room, just what I liked, room for vision and creativity. The dark paneled walls would be a striking backdrop for the white linen tablecloths and chair covers that I would use. The wedding ceremony would be held over an hour away from our home on a Saturday evening in tiny Sharpsburg. We left early on a Friday morning, our destination the hotel where the reception would be hosted.

Our trip began early for the weekend events that were planned. As we pulled down the driveway in our car, about eight in the morning, I still remember that last look at our home and my eyes rested on a special tree. The sugar maple that my mother helped me plant when we moved in our house some twenty years before, stood in blazing glory. It was as red as I have ever seen it and was symbolic of the wedding that had been planned by Jess and Heather to honor their favorite time of year. The tree, resplendent in its glory, left its print on my heart as I will always remember the branches that looked like flames burning, a testament to the beauty of life. Mother and I had planted that tree some twenty two years before. Jess was only eleven years old. He was a man now and about to begin his own life as a married man. He had certainly survived the trauma of his first birthday party and had progressed in the following years without incident. I had survived as well into a proud and confident mother.

Decorating for the rehearsal dinner would be a challenge, as I also had a bridesmaid luncheon to attend. The hours were precious and time was a commodity on that day. I wanted the rehearsal dinner to reflect the same love and care that I had given Katie on her special day. I only had about fifty guests to entertain, but I can attest that setting up a buffet requires just as much work and presentation as for a much larger number. Its success was critical to the effect I hoped to achieve. The guests' tables would be covered in the white cloths that made the room come alive. Silver chargers were to be used with white plates and napkins. Arrangements were made with live green ivy cascading down the sides of glass containers, crowned with red apples. Tiny white pumpkins completed the arrangements. Candles were glowing in the red apples that were carved to hold them. The table for the bridal party would be in reverse, with red cloths and white napkins. It was the picture of fall and the room was soon transformed into a beautiful and gracious setting. The catered Cajun meal included fresh shrimp fried on site and was not complete without the outstanding gumbo that was devoured. Bananas Foster was the hit of the evening, but the bread pudding with rum sauce was my favorite. It was a wonderful affair and I was thrilled with its success. Somehow, minus my involvement in the food preparation, I felt just as tired and just as spent when it was all over.

The wedding was beautiful and the reception equally so. What a wonderful treat to enjoy a beautiful reception that was planned by my future daughter- in-law and her mother. Careful time and consideration had been taken to make the reception equally significant for both families. This time I was gaining a daughter. I already had another son, so this was new for me. Katie finally had a sister and it felt good. She had been handpicked, literally, by Katie who had a class with her in college. Then they had become roommates. My firstborn had found his soul mate and he had chosen well, along with a little help from his sister.

Patti, the perfect hostess, played her role again, driving about fifty miles to again help her grateful friend. My friends have always been there for me, but more importantly for me, I pledge to do the same for them. They have kept me grounded. What a sweet promise that God has given as he commands in Proverbs 27:9 Perfume and incense bring joy to the heart, and the pleasantness of a friend springs from their heartfelt advice; those words – to find comfort and solace in our friends – his promise.

And now that I have brought you to the departure of two my children from my nest, I realize that I have not spoken much of motherhood. I feel myself deprived of the eloquent words that encompass the sheer significance of being a mother. Furthermore, no one could have prepared me for the magnitude of motherhood, and for that matter, I am not alone. From the moment you hold your child, your flesh and blood, for the first time, that child is bonded to your soul. It is beyond your imagination, when they are born, that someday they will leave you behind; no matter how much you prepare them to make their way into this world.

The one day of the year that you can claim to be yours, if only in your heart is Mother's Day. And so it is, if you are lucky, your children will come home to honor you, their mother, on your special day. For me, the day seems like minutes, and soon they must leave to go back to their world, and each and every time they leave - emptiness. Don't get me wrong, I am grateful for every moment I spend with my children. But, no one told me that when they come and go, they leave a void. Sometimes I feel lost, even for a few hours after my children visit, and sensibility rushes in to bring me back to reality and gratefulness. Can any man feel the depth of that love or is that only consigned to women? I wonder? Do you ever really get over missing your children after they are grown and gone? For me that is not an option. When they come home, it feels – well, let's just say, "It feels right."

Speaking of home, when I was growing up, many people referred to the home that they had grown up in as a "home place". Great value was placed on the shelter that housed a family, to the extent that sentimentality prevailed in preserving that sacred structure. Not anymore. It is not unusual for people today to occupy several homes over their lifetime. That was not what we wanted for our children. Today, I still want our home to be a place that our children can always feel "at home" – a place for tradition. I still' have the notion that I can resurrect the loss of Sunday dinner at Grandma's house – a haven to escape the hustle and bustle of this new world. But reality hits me square in the face.

Quite frequently I find myself driving to one of my children's homes, the miles stealing from me. The miles take away the gift of time. My children all live just far enough away to eliminate the convenience of a frequent visit. So now time becomes my loss, as convenience for them rests in my willingness to drive to see them. But, who I am to complain? They could live far away or in another state. Notice I make reference to the trips that I make. In an effort to balance family time with work, school and responsibilities at home, a trip to the home place seems to be harder and harder to achieve for my children.

In the words of Millard Lyman Jones, better known as DeDaddy, "You have got to have air castles!" I will continue to have the air castles that I have created – hopes that someday my children will come full circle to a place they can still call home and the realization of how important it is for their children, my grandchildren. I will wait patiently and always count my blessings, grateful that I have my children and grandchildren and the air castles of my heart.

The Gift

The camaraderie of friendship is the reward, although the sacrifice of the heart can sometimes be quite painful. For in friendship, the magnitude of a friend's joy and pain will find ownership in your heart. There is no refrain. The heart is committed and for me the measure of true friendship lies in the valleys that we endure as friends. Sometimes those valleys might include the death of a loved one - to the degree that no mother or father should ever have to endure - the death of a child. When we extend our heart to a friend, the tentacles of love do not just wrap themselves around that being, they become intertwined **with those hearts that are immersed within them.**

Death has come far too often in several of my friend's lives in the worst kind of way – a child. Sometimes it was without warning and sometimes through years of a debilitating illness. Either way, it is nevertheless shocking and intensely painful watching from the outside. I cannot even imagine what it is like to feel the pain as a parent losing a child. I just know that as a friend, it has been excruciating.

I was in a department store when I learned of the death of a dear friend's daughter. Upon learning the news, I was so distraught and desperate. I found myself in the maze of the housewares that I normally found so enticing – my eyes saw nothing. Then something caught my attention. It was a replica of a ballerina, gently and eloquently lifted on pointe, with arms extended like a butterfly. She was ready to take flight and at that moment I knew. God spoke to me and the peace and calm surrounded me. The broken body that I was grieving for had taken flight and was anew in heaven. She had been a ballerina, dancing so eloquently in her younger years and now was dancing on clouds. I knew and felt it just as if she whispered in my ear. My duty now was to console the mother whose pain I could not imagine. So ironic is friendship, for even in our darkest hour, the inconsolable becomes consoler. I learned later that evening she had wanted to spare me, dreading to tell me the sad news.

When I arrived at her home, we went through the ritual of crying and hugging one another, making senseless conversation for hours. Then, we were alone. It was scary and I felt so helpless. We sat on the couch, locked in each other's embrace and I shamelessly cried deep sobbing cries, failing miserably in my mission of consoler. We both cried. I was a failure, but our tears brought us both a level of peace that we could tolerate. We sat there until the wee hours of the morning, me at a loss of words that I felt worthy of speaking. In my pitiful effort of consolation, I knew that my presence was enough for her. My tears had flowed freely, liberating me from the chest crushing weight that I understood was minute compared to what my friend felt.

As we sat there, she said something that I felt was quite profound. She spoke of my "gift". In her estimation, my "gift" was the ability to feel compassion as though the experience was my own. I certainly did not feel "gifted". I just felt empty and void, helpless and grateful that the compassion she spoke of was something I could give in that heart wrenching moment, compassion that now consumed my soul.

I had not known my friend's daughter on a deep personal level, but it did not matter. I had known her mother for years and she is just as dear to me as a sister. And her child was my child too. All of the memories and stories that her mother and I had shared made her mine. I could not separate the two of them, mother nor daughter. They were one and the same.

Over the years, several of my friends have lost a child and their loss has been none the less shocking or painful, but this one was so personal for me. The loss of this beautiful and wonderful girl touched deeper. Perhaps, because my own daughter had just given birth to my first grandson, continuing the cycle of life. Life - motherhood had given my friend and me both the opportunity to be a part in God's creation, the ultimate human experience for us both, and now my daughter. In doing so, we all had accepted the responsibility of shaping another human life. With it comes intense and unconditional love. With it comes lifelong pleasure and for those friends of mine who have lost; a final sorrow, woven with eternal joy - their lives richer for the experience. I hope that I never experience that final sorrow and would not wish it on anyone, accepting my "gift" as a compassionate friend, as that - a gift.

Meet Recoursah

So in this school of life and to all of the players, the teachers, friends, family and anyone who has helped to mold me into the person that I have become, I salute you. There are too many people to mention, too many stories to tell and I humble myself before all of them and you in my attempt to enlighten all of this southern girl's hopes and dreams. I will try to sum it all up through my introduction of Recoursah.

Once again, I am spiraled back in time, sitting at the dining room table on Farris Avenue in East Point. I am hanging on every word that the aunts have to say. To the best of my recollection, it had to be Hiawassee, Jean and perhaps Sue who were present. They were the smokers.

Rings of smoke ascend through the air, drifting nonchalantly and hanging in a heavy cloud, surrounding the oblivious of the dangers of that nicotine fix. As usual after a meal, the sisters sit at the table for an indefinite length of time conversing with one another as families do. I am all ears, hearing the praises of my sister Jan and her unusual beauty. They speak of her beautiful blonde hair. The genes of my father were strong and he had made his mark. My sister's high cheekbones were of his own, not to mention the blonde curly hair that framed her cherubic face; the sea green eyes that completed her looks - from my mother. Someone, I am not sure who, chimes in and begins to compliment my own fair looks, and the promise of what the future will hold for me, declaring that I will be a beauty and will surpass my sister in looks in the future. As I listen, I feel some satisfaction in knowing that one of them is my champion and has confidence that I will turn out to be pretty someday. Even then, I had already felt the sting of rejection at school. I was thin and my fine hair likewise. It was a mousy brown with a reddish tint. I had big blue eyes and a scattering of freckles. I was called skinny.

That was my first awareness of the beauty of a sister that I have always adored and I felt proud, not envious then or now. I know now that she was a gift that only God could have given to me. I am sure that He breathed life into her to make a difference in my life and surely to those that know and love her.

158

Jan was born the year before Gwen died and shortly before she found out that she had cancer. I am further convinced that when God took Gwen away, he in his infinite wisdom sought to take away some of the pain that my mother endured. Surely, my mother was able to negate some of the sense of loss as she watched her daughters play and love one another, then and now, as we have always done – a reminder of her cherished sister.

I never felt animosity toward Jan and her beauty. She was my playmate and my best friend. I was her guardian and always felt a sense of responsibility toward her. She, after all, was younger. She was my charge and with the three years that stood between us, I felt that I had the license to be in control. I never gave a second thought what my role would be to Jan and neither did she, now that I think of it. She and I were always together. Of course I had friends, but when I went away to visit, I knew that my sister would be waiting there when I would arrive home.

Those magical days of summer that I spoke of earlier were all made possible because of my sister. I was her hero, but I wanted to emulate her carefree demeanor. She did not care about things that did not matter. I was serious, she was free spirited. I was in control, but my perfectionism controlled me. I wanted to be more like her – laid back and easygoing. It was not in the cards, but she kept me grounded. She loved people and animals alike - encompassing love. She kissed our dogs and hugged them and her compassion for them was unequaled. She was beautiful, both inside and out. When nighttime fell and we climbed into our twin beds in the room we shared, Jan and I, barely able to move, lined our dolls by our sides, so they would never feel forgotten. If we forgot one, we would feel so bad that we hopped up to retrieve it, making our way back to the bed, snuggling it close by our side, whether we had room or not. They were loved!

The dolls could not speak for themselves, but we both loved and took care of them just like our own children today. One of her dolls, I remember so well, perhaps the only one that will never leave my mind. I don't exactly recall where Jan acquired the doll, but I do know her name. Her name was Recoursah! What and where could anyone come up with such a name? I recall asking her that very question, but don't remember the answer. Perhaps it was derived from the word corset; after all, my grandmother wore a corset. I just know that I was in awe of her creativity and much impressed. The name was really odd and I did not much care for it, but it really didn't matter. Recently, upon jogging her memory, she said that she just wanted a name that no one else had used before. I am certain she was successful!

So now you may wonder, what impact did Recoursah have to do with my life and what influence could she have on my love of cooking? The answer is quite simple. Recoursah is representative of the carefree days that Jan and I spent, just loving our dolls and dreaming of the day, when we would be real mothers – nurturing our own families and caring for them. And for us, it was a nurturing of our souls as we witnessed the love and devotion of our family as they prepared even the most humble of meals.

We experienced humility through our mother and the matriarch of our family, Mimi, who loved the very trees that rose above her and the wind that made the leaves put on a show just for her entertainment. She did not long for riches, she was content with the riches that surrounded her every day, simple pleasures that only the astute heart can appreciate. She knew the secret to life was God and family, and loving them without reserve. No holds barred, just true unconditional love. She taught us love and compassion that could have only been acquired from her trials and tribulations. So when Jan and I were in our fantasy world of dolls and imagination, the focus was on love of family and for both of us, the love of a sister. Recoursah – a doll - a symbol of influence for two little girls who would grow up and become mothers, but forever sisters.

It was then as it is with us now, somewhere in between the devotion that both of us have for our respective families and our endless love for them, we share an encompassing bond that only exists in what I believe is perfect sisterhood. The bond is a cloak that we have worn through all the seasons of our lives and from which we draw our strength, as women, mothers and sisters.

Perfect sisterhood cannot be taught or achieved, rather built on shared life experiences. I am convinced however; that it can be achieved between women, even when there is no biological bond, for not everyone is lucky enough to have a sister. It is the joy and happiness, the love and sometimes the pain we as women share. Pain can be just as profound to one as it is to the other, but the cloak will never feel too heavy or cumbersome to wear - the measure of perfect sisterhood. So it was when my sister had her first labor pain. I awakened in the middle of the night with thoughts of her and her first unborn child to come, and I arose and looked out the window in search of the answer my heart had already given. She would be a mother soon. And when motherhood has sometimes become so overwhelming beyond our expectations, we have found comfort in each other, finding solace in the reassurance that we share a sister's love.

The older sister, the one in charge and the one always in control has been brought to her knees and humbled by the dear and gentle sister that has my complete admiration. Jan is the one who along with my mother, cared for my ailing father the last years of his life. Forget that she was raising four children of her own. I find myself in awe of her sometimes when she speaks with eloquent expression, opening my own eyes to her profound wisdom. She has charm and charisma in a quiet and beautiful way, that others feel drawn to her. She has complete and total faith in what God has in store for her and a trusting spirit.

In good times and bad, prevail we shall, just as we did on those late evenings of childhood as we ran breathlessly down the street, trying to escape from the abandoned house that loomed in the dark, to find solace in the comfort of our home. And to the dolls that needed our love and attention – our children for the moment and one with the name of Recoursah.

Recoursah is the sum of what our childhood dreams were made of – loving our families and then creating our own. She was just a doll, made of rubber, with molded curls of that same substance, and eyes that opened and closed. We were her guardians and loved her with the same care and concern that was breathed into both of our souls. From those hot sultry nights on Fair Street, nights that forged memories in the refuge of our minds, of sisters who were not complete without one another – we became women – southern women. One trait that was taught to us, one that has trumped all others is compassion. It is what separates the good from evil. If there is one thing that I will be forever grateful is that we were raised with a sympathetic heart and a humble spirit.

And so it is with compassion, that when we want to show our love for friends and family, the sacred kitchen beckons. *We cook for love, we cook for joy. We cook when death knocks on doors, our*

161

hearts full of sorrow - when we can do no more, than offer the repast of our hearts. There is no need for declarations; the gesture is worth a thousand words. In joy and in sorrow, the kitchen is our haven and our refuge to provide nourishment to the souls of those we love.

Recoursah is representative to me of the best that life has to offer, hope for the future and comfort of family. If choosing to love and nourish your family is your ultimate goal, can there ever be one more worthy?

Some of those loved ones left me one by one, but not without leaving their dreams and aspirations that inspire me to continue my own life as an empathetic mother, sister and now grandmother. The aunts and the grandmothers, the dolls that are now nameless, except for Recoursah are gone forever from my life. I will always aspire to become one of them, always loving and giving more – intertwined with *Hearts Immersed Within.*

Wishes....like magic were elusive and intangible, but we held them tight and smothered our hearts with their hope.

Revelation

As you peruse the menus and recipes on the following pages, the tidbits of their origin weave a story of faith, family and friends. Don't be surprised when you also find there are *Hearts Immersed Within* them.

After a lifetime of inspiration and transformation, it is with great pleasure that I have revealed to you some of the recipes born from the women in my life. I have shared their influences that have made me love the heart of the kitchen and all the rewards it has to offer. Yes, my kitchen has a heart and I can feel the love as I prepare the food that I know will make my friends and family happy, creating memories that will last a lifetime. Just as a song can bring back the emotions of times gone by, the sensory of taste can do the same.

I have compiled for you an assortment of menus and recipes featuring dishes for all occasions. They were selected with great care. Each and every recipe that I have chosen has a special meaning. I cannot claim to have created most of the recipes, but have become their caretaker and give credit to each who has shared their gift with me. I have only been their honored keeper. During my catering years, I was not at liberty to reveal the recipes that garnered me my reputation. However, my cooking prowess has not been measured by the recipes alone, but by my most fortunate years of training. We have all been taught that practice makes perfect. That old adage is never more applicable than when cooking in the kitchen. Having said that, don't be discouraged if a recipe does not turn out as you would have wished the first time. Continue to forge ahead in your kitchen endeavors and the rewards will be yours. You are not only creating a dish for consumption, but you are giving a part of yourself.

Relish Everyday Meals
at their Sunday Best

PoppySeed Chicken
Steamed White Rice
Oven Baked Asparagus
Sour Cream Drop Biscuits

Poppyseed Chicken

This is a simple, but satisfying recipe used for young beginners in my cooking class. I taught stove-top techniques with an emphasis on safety.

Tip: Always read the entire recipe before you begin your preparations.

Pre-heat oven to 350 degrees

6 chicken breasts
2 cans of cream of chicken soup
1 small carton of sour cream (8 oz.)
1 stick of margarine
1 sleeve of buttery crackers
1 tsp. poppyseed
Salt and pepper to taste

Place chicken breasts in a large stock pot and cover with water. Bring to a boil on high heat. Reduce heat to medium low and cover. Simmer between 45 minutes to an hour until breasts are fork tender. Remove from pot and de-bone. Cut into bite size pieces.

Grease a 2 quart casserole dish with cooking spray. Place cooked chicken in the bottom of the casserole and distribute evenly. Sprinkle lightly with salt and pepper. In a medium size mixing bowl, combine soup and sour cream with a spatula. Pour over the chicken. Melt margarine in a microwave safe dish on high for 1 minute. Place the crackers in a zip lock bag and crush with hands by rolling between open hands and then add margarine, using the same motion to distribute the margarine. Place the crackers in a uniform manner over the top of the chicken casserole. Sprinkle with the poppy seed. Bake at 350 degrees for thirty minutes or until nice and bubbly. Serve over steamed white rice.

*Boneless and skinless chicken may be used by following the same cooking procedure.

Oven Baked Asparagus

Pre-heat oven to 400 degrees

1 bunch of asparagus
Olive oil
Salt and Pepper to taste or your favorite seasoning

Wash and trip asparagus spears. Spears can be trimmed by snapping the ends of each individual stalk 1 to 2 inches from the bottom. The spear will easily break where the tender section begins by gently bending the spear, working from the bottom. Place the spears on a cookie sheet and lightly sprinkle with olive oil to coat. Season the asparagus with salt and pepper or your favorite seasoning. Bake for 10 to 15 minutes until the spears are tender, but firm.
*You may sprinkle with fresh grated parmesan cheese and return to the oven for 1 to 2 minutes or until slightly melted.

Sour Cream Drop Biscuits

This recipe is absolute ease and you will be the star of the show. As Cousin Sarah (Sà – ruh) calls them, "Done N' Buttered," you will see why. They taste like a biscuit that has already been buttered.

2 c. self-rising flour
1 c. sour cream
2 sticks margarine, softened

Place flour in a medium bowl. Add the margarine and work into the flour with a gloved hand until smooth. Add the sour cream and continue combining until smooth and dough forms. Drop by heaping tablespoons onto cookie sheet lightly greased with cooking spray. You may use a muffin tin or a mini muffin tin works well. If using a muffin tin, fill half full. Bake 15 to 20 minutes until lightly brown. Serve immediately.

Yields 18 to 24 muffins or biscuits; 36 to 48 mini muffins.

Pork Chops and
Brown Rice
Cabbage Stir Fry
Yeast Muffin Surprise

Pork Chops and Brown Rice

Preheat oven to 300 degrees

6 to 8 boneless pork chops
2 c. uncooked rice
1 stick of margarine
1 can of beef consume soup
1 soup can of water
1 tsp. Worchester sauce
1 tsp. black pepper
1 large jar of sliced mushrooms

In a large size skillet, quick brown chops in a small amount of cooking spray on medium high heat. Remove the chops from the skillet and set aside.

In a medium size microwavable bowl, melt margarine for one minute on high. Remove from microwave and stir in soup, rice, black pepper, Worchester sauce and mushrooms. Pour into a greased 13 X 9 casserole that has been coated with cooking spray. Layer chops on to top of rice mixture. Bake at 300 degrees for one hour.

Cabbage Stir Fry

This is a great side dish for pork. However, it is good with beef or chicken. The celery, pepper and onions give the cabbage a creative and unique flavor.

1 medium cabbage
1 medium onion
4 stalks of celery hearts
1 medium bell pepper
Vegetable oil
Salt and Black Pepper

Wash the cabbage and slice in wedges from top to bottom on all four sides, then across the bottom, leaving the core. Using a cutting board, place each wedge, cut side down and slice lengthwise in thin slices, creating an angel hair effect in the slices. Then, cut down the center of all slices at once. Continue with each wedge until all cabbage had been sliced. Use enough oil to coat the bottom of a 3 to 4 quart skillet. Add the cabbage to the pan. Quarter and slice the onion into very thin slices. Cut the celery stalks into thin slices, cross-wise of the stalk, and the bell pepper in small thin ½ inch sizes. Add the cut and sliced ingredients to the cabbage, stirring to mix all ingredients. Heat vegetables on medium high, stirring until the vegetables begin to sizzle and steam. Cabbage is naturally full of moisture. Reduce heat and cook covered on low to medium heat, until the vegetables are soft, about 20 minutes. You will need to stir frequently to distribute the oil. Add salt and pepper to taste as the cabbage mixture begins to wilt.

Yeast Muffin Surprise

Pre-heat oven to 400 degrees

4 c. self- rising flour
1/4 c. sugar
1/2 c. very warm water
1 envelope active dry yeast
1 ½ c. milk
2 sticks of margarine

In a medium size microwavable bowl, melt margarine on high for 1 minute. Remove from microwave. In a small mixing bowl, mix yeast with warm water until dissolved. Stir yeast mixture with a wire whisk into the melted margarine until evenly distributed. Add the milk and stir until well blended. Blend in flour and sugar, stirring to form a soft dough that resembles a very thick batter. Dough will appear somewhat lumpy. Drop by heaping tablespoons into greased muffin tin until half full. Bake in oven for 15 to 20 minutes until golden brown. Yields 24 muffins.

*I frequently cut this recipe in half to serve for evening meals. You may make the entire recipe and store the remaining dough in the refrigerator for 2 to 3 days.

Country Fried Steak
and Gravy
Steamed White Rice
Cole Slaw
Buttermilk Biscuits

Country Fried Steak and Gravy

4 to 6 pieces of top round steak that has been cubed
2 c. self-rising flour
2 tsp. Lawry's Seasoned Salt
2 tsp. black pepper
1 c. milk
2 to 3 c. water
Peanut oil

Rinse cubed steak with water and gently pat with paper toweling. Place flour in a gallon zip lock bag. Add seasonings. Close bag and shake till seasonings are blended. Pour milk in a small shallow bowl. Dip steak pieces individually into the milk, making sure to coat both sides and then drop into the flour, repeating the process until all pieces are in the bag. Close the bag and shake until the pieces are thoroughly coated. Remove the battered steak and place on paper toweling. You may place in the refrigerator if you are not ready to fry the meat.

Pour ½ inch of oil in an electric fry pan or large skillet on cook top, Heat on medium high heat until the oil sizzles when a pinch of flour is dropped into it. Place the battered meat into the oil one piece at a time. Reduce heat immediately to medium low. If you will notice, the meat will be browning rapidly around the edges. Turn the meat over. Cook the meat until medium brown on both sides and fork tender. You may increase the heat as you are ready to remove the meat. This will prevent the absorption of oil, cooking some of the oil out of the meat. Using a meat fork, remove the meat from the skillet individually, allowing to drip excess oil over the skillet as meat is being removed. (Extinguish heat if the grease seems to be getting too.) Place meat on paper toweling for additional absorption of oil. Remove the skillet from the heat or turn off electric skillet as soon as the meat has been removed.

Return skillet to medium high heat. With a spoon, scrape drippings from the bottom of pan. Place 2 heaping tablespoons of flour in the skillet. Using a wire whisk, stir the mixture rapidly until flour has turned a medium to dark brown. Slowly add 2 cups of water, continuing to stir constantly. As soon as the gravy starts to thicken, reduce heat to simmer. Add one medium onion sliced thin. Cover and simmer about 15 minutes or until onion is tender. You may add the additional cup of water to make thin gravy, stirring in slowly for desired consistency. Steak may be added back to the gravy if desired or served separately. Rice or mashed potatoes are a great side to compliment the meat and gravy. A green vegetable of your choice completes the meal.

Cole Slaw

Cole slaw is a wonderful accompaniment for a variety of main courses. It serves to temper some of the greasiness found in fried or spicy foods. You will find another version listed under the Sinfully Southern section labeled Fish Slaw. It is equally as good.

1 large cabbage
1 large carrot, grated
1 tbl. celery seed
Mayonnaise – use sparingly until quantity desired
Sweet relish, drained and added to taste
Salt and pepper to taste

Wash cabbage and slice in wedges from top to bottom on all four sides, then across the bottom, removing the core. Using a cutting board, place each wedge, cut side down and slice lengthwise in thin slices, creating an angel hair effect in the slices. Continue with each wedge until all cabbage had been sliced. Place cabbage and grated carrot in a large mixing bowl. Using a hand chopper, chop the slices of cabbage until it is a coarse consistency. If an electric chopper is used, it will create a watery slaw and the cabbage may need to be drained with a colander. Add the relish and celery seed. Stir in the mayonnaise, sparingly, only using enough to lightly coat the cabbage, as the moisture from the cabbage will increase. Serves 8.

Buttermilk Biscuits

After years of making biscuits, I must make a confession. I make a big mess. No matter how hard I have tried, the mess continues. I watched my mother make biscuits in her wooden bowl, seamlessly as if it were an art. I never could seem to make biscuits taste good, until I started using this recipe. I find myself adding flour to my hands after each biscuit is formed – good luck in this endeavor, regardless the biscuits will be worth it. Keep a wet paper towel handy and you will be fine.

Tip: For light biscuits, handle as little as possible once the dough has been mixed.

Pre-heat oven to 400 degrees

½ c. of margarine, cold
2 c. self-rising flour
1 c. whole buttermilk

Place the flour in a medium sized mixing bowl. Cut the margarine in with a pastry cutter or use gloved hand, incorporating it in until the margarine has been distributed throughout and pieces are the size of a dime. Add the buttermilk and gently blend with spoon or hand, until all the flour has been incorporated and dough is formed. (Too much flour in the dough can make biscuits too heavy.) With floured hands, pinch off dough in golf ball sizes and roll in floured palms until smooth. Place biscuits on greased baking pan and pat with fingers to make a ½ inch thick biscuit. Repeat process, placing the biscuits on the pan, so that they touch. Allow biscuits to sit on the counter for about 30 minutes, if time allows, for a nice smooth appearance when baked.

*If desired, place the dough on a floured pastry sheet and roll the dough out with a floured rolling pin making a circle 12 inches in diameter and about ½ inch in thickness. Use a biscuit cutter to cut 12 biscuits. You may need to reshape the dough into a ball and roll out again to make the dozen biscuits.

Relish Special Occasions
Will you? I do...

...and a family too!

Engagement Celebration

Jean's Boneless Breaded Chicken

Simple Squash

Marinated Vegetable Salad

Crusty French Bakery Bread

The Perfect Chocolate Cake

Jean's Boneless Breaded Chicken

Pre-heat oven to 200 degrees

1 ½ c. bread crumbs (day old bread, processed in blender/food processor until fine)
½ c. fresh parsley, chopped fine
3 egg whites
¼ c. vermouth
1 stick clarified butter*
8 boneless/skinless chicken breasts
1 lemon, sliced
1 c. sliced toasted almonds

Toast almonds in a small amount of butter in a large skillet, stirring on medium heat until golden brown, about five minutes. Remove from heat and then from the skillet. Set almonds aside to cool.

Prepare crumbs by using blender/food processor and place in a shallow bowl. Chop parsley in blender and stir into bread crumbs.

Place chicken breasts between wax paper/plastic wrap individually, using a wooden mallet, pound chicken until ½ inch thickness.

Beat the 3 egg whites with a wire whisk until foamy. Dip chicken in egg whites and then into the crumb mixture, pressing the crumbs into the chicken, to form a breading. Let cool on a cookie sheet in the refrigerator for at least 30 minutes. Fry chicken in large skillet on medium high heat in the clarified butter. The process should take about 15 minutes – 7 to 8 minutes on each side of the chicken or until both sides are golden brown. Remove the pieces individually with tongs, shaking butter residue as they are removed. Remove skillet from heat. Place chicken onto a warm oven proof platter and put in the pre-heated oven.

Slice the lemon thin and sauté in the remaining butter. Remove from heat and arrange on warming chicken. Return platter to oven. Add vermouth and chicken broth to butter, cooking until bubbly.

Remove chicken from oven once again and pour the sauce over the chicken, garnish with toasted almonds.

*Clarified butter is made by removing the milk solid and water. It can be cooked at a higher heat without burning. Clarified butter can be kept longer without going rancid.

Melt butter slowly, and then allow it to sit until it separates. Skim off the foam that rises. Gently pour the butter off of the milk solids. You will have rendered about 6 tablespoons of clarified butter from one stick which equals 8 tablespoons or ½ cup.

Simple Squash

2 to 4 lbs. yellow squash
1 large onion
1 c. water
¼ c. bacon grease
½ stick of margarine

Wash and cut squash slices, removing ends. Remove skin from onion and trim on both ends. Cut in half from top to bottom. Place cut side down and thinly slice each half, holding the slices together. Then, cut the slices down the middle. Place onions and squash in a 2 qt. boiler. Add ½ c. of water. Bring to a boil. Reduce heat to simmer and cook until squash is fork tender, about 15 minutes. Onions will be tender. There will be a small amount of water when squash are cooked. Remove from heat. Chop squash and onion together with a hand chopper, in a mixing bowl. Add the bacon drippings and margarine. (If you choose, you may delete either one or both) Return to the skillet and simmer on low until most of the liquid is absorbed. Cover and turn off heat until ready to serve.

The Perfect Chocolate Cake

1 c. un-sifted, unsweetened cocoa
2 c. boiling water
2 ¾ c. sifted, all-purpose flour
½ tsp. salt
2 tsp. baking soda
1 tsp. baking powder
1 c. butter or margarine, softened
2 ½ c. granulated sugar
4 eggs
1 ½ tsp. vanilla extract

Frosting:
1 pkg. (6 oz.) semi-sweet chocolate pieces
½ c. light cream
2 ½ c. un-sifted confectioner's sugar
½ c. butter or margarine

Filling:
1 c. heavy cream
¼ c. un-sifted confectioner's sugar
1 tsp. vanilla extract

Pre-heat oven to 350 degrees

For layers: In a medium bowl, combine cocoa with boiling water, mixing with a wire whisk until smooth. Let cool completely. Sift together flour, soda, salt and baking powder. In large bowl of electric mixer, at high speed, beat butter, sugar, eggs and vanilla together until light, scraping bowl occasionally with rubber spatula – about 5 minutes. Adjust mixer to low speed, beginning and ending with the flour, beat in fourths alternately with thirds of the cocoa mixture. Do not overbeat, mixing only until mixture is well blended after each addition. Grease and lightly flour three 9 X 1½ inch layer cake pans. Pour a third of the mixture in each pan. Bake about 20 to 25 minutes, or until the center springs back when lightly touched.

Remove from oven and cool on a wire rack for about 10 minutes. Remove from pans by inserting a dull knife between outer edges of cake layer to loosen it from edge of pan. Repeat the process to remove the remaining layers. Turn out on parchment paper and allow the layers to cool. While layers are baking, prepare as filling and frosting as follows:

Filling:
Beat heavy cream on high speed of mixer until thick, adding sugar and vanilla while continuing to beat. Continue beating until the mixture is thick and will not loosen when the bowl is inverted slightly. Place in refrigerator to cool.

Frosting:
In a medium size saucepan, combine chocolate pieces, light cream, and butter. Cook over medium heat until smooth, stirring constantly. Remove from heat. With a wire whisk, blend in confectioner's sugar. Place saucepan in a larger bowl, half filled with ice and continue whisking until the chocolate holds shape.

On a cake plate, spoon a small amount of the *frosting* to form a circle the size of cake layer. Place one of the layers, top side down on the frosting. Spread half of the *filling* over the layer. Place the second layer, top side down and spread with the remainder of the *filling*. Place the remaining layer top side up to complete stacking of layers. With a spatula, spread the cake *frosting* to cover sides and top of cake, making sure that *filling* is covered on the sides of cake.

Aunt Dale's Marinated Veggie Salad

Aunt Dale made a lasting impression with her fabulous dinner at which a wonderful lasagna casserole was served. The salad that was served took top honors in my book. I prepare this salad with Italian food, but also serve it to guests as an unexpected "surprise salad". I am so thankful for the recipe and its unusual taste.

Tip: The vegetables in this salad may be marinated overnight. I encourage doing so, as it will save time and will be so helpful to achieve a stress-free dinner party.

1 12 oz. jar of marinated artichoke hearts
1 cup of grape tomatoes, halved
1 ripe avocado, diced
1 medium cucumber, diced
1 head of iceberg lettuce
Your favorite Italian Dressing

Combine first 4 ingredients in a medium size mixing bowl. Cover and marinate for 2 hours or more in the refrigerator. Wash and tear the lettuce into bite size pieces. Add the marinated vegetables to the lettuce and toss just before serving. Sprinkle with dressing. Serves 6 to 8.

Meet the Bride Tea

Creamy Chicken Salad

Cream Cheese Olive Sandwiches

Cheese Pecan Wafers

Poppyseed Bread

Dorrie's Pasta Salad

Allison's Almond Tea

Creamy Chicken Salad

For a tea party sensation, trim crust from the cinnamon swirl bread and then spread softened margarine on both sides of the bread. Press each slice into muffin cups and bake in a 300 degree oven until lightly brown, about 15 to 20 minutes. Remove and cool. Fill with chicken salad and garnish with parsley or celery leaf.

Tip: Serve this salad on store bought cinnamon swirl bread that has been spread with margarine and toasted on griddle for a special treat.

6 boneless chicken breasts
3 ribs of celery hearts, diced thin
½ c. sweet pickle relish
1 tsp. cracked black pepper
1 c. mayonnaise
½ c. applesauce

Cover the chicken breast with water in a medium stock pot. Bring to a boil over high heat, reduce heat to low and simmer for 1 hour or until fork tender. Remove chicken from the pot and place in a medium size mixing bowl. Discard the broth or freeze for future use. Allow the chicken to cool and using a gloved hand, tear the chicken into a stringy texture. Add the remaining ingredients, blending well with hand. Refrigerate for at least one hour before serving.

Variations:
*Add ½ c. pecans or ½ c. toasted almonds to the above recipe if desired.
*Honey mustard can be substituted for the applesauce
*¾ cup of either craisins, sliced grapes or granny smith apples cubed can be substituted or can be in addition to the pickles.
*Trimmed crusts from the cinnamon bread may be reserved for a breakfast treat. Heat waffle iron to high heat. Place leftover crust in a layer and then top with squeezable margarine. Close lid and wait for the aroma to permeate the air. Remove from the waffle iron when lightly brown and toasted. Great with coffee.

Dorrie's Pasta Salad

1 16.5 oz. box multi-color twist pasta
6 oz. Italian Dressing with Romano Cheese
5 oz. sharp cheddar cheese, cubed
1 small can of sliced black olives, drained
½ cup mayonnaise
1 8 oz. container of feta cheese
2 pickling cucumbers, peeled and cubed
2 small tomatoes, chopped into ½ inch cubes, or
8 oz. grape tomatoes, halved

Cook and drain pasta as directed on box. Transfer to a large mixing bowl. Pour dressing over the pasta while warm and stir gently to distribute. Add the next four ingredients, again stirring gently. Cover and refrigerate 2 to 3 hours or overnight. Add the cucumbers and tomatoes just before serving.

Allison's Almond Tea

This is a refreshing drink that can be served at both luncheons and showers. It is not too sweet and pairs well with lunch and dessert.

2 qts. unsweetened tea
4 c. water
1 c. sugar
1 tsp. vanilla flavoring
1tsp. almond flavoring
2 qts. unsweetened pineapple juice

Bring water to a boil. Stir in sugar and flavorings. Remove from heat and allow to cool. In a gallon container, blend tea and cooled mixture. Refrigerate until you are ready to serve. In a punch bowl, combine tea and pineapple juice. Place an ice ring in the mixture. An easy ring is made from water, sliced lemons, oranges and limes or your choice placed in a Bundt pan and frozen. Serve punch over ice.

Cheese Pecan Wafers

I found a recipe that was similar to cheese straws that is very simple, but has the same taste. These wafers are a great accompaniment when serving chicken salad and mirror the selection at *Rich's Magnolia Room* that I loved so much! They are similar to cheese straws, but not as light. They are equally as good. Yum!

Pre-heat oven to 400 degrees

½ c. pecans
½ lb. margarine, softened
½ lb. sharp cheddar cheese, grated
2 c. plain flour
1 Tbl. sugar
½ tsp. salt

Cream the margarine and cheese until well blended with a gloved hand. Add nuts and the dry ingredients and mix well, forming into dough. Refrigerate for 15 minutes to achieve stiff dough. With a gloved hand, divide the dough in half and roll into two logs, the circumference of a silver dollar. Place the logs on plastic wrap that has been greased with cooking spray. Wrap the dough and place in refrigerator for at least 15 more minutes. Remove from refrigerator and cut into ¼ inch slices. Place on a cookie sheet and bake at 400 degrees until lightly brown, about 8 to 10 minutes. Be very careful to monitor the wafers as the bottoms will brown very quickly. Allow to cool before serving or before storing in an airtight container. Yields about 4 dozen wafers.

*Dough can be stored for up to one week in refrigerator, but will never last that long – the wafers will be baked much sooner!

Poppyseed Bread

What can I say about Sarah? She married my father-in-law's first cousin and has been well known for her graciousness and hospitality in both our family and in the Middle Georgia town of Hawkinsville. If not tied for first, I would have to say that Sarah has contributed almost as many recipes to my collection as Mary Frances. Her reputation in Hawkinsville is synonymous with the word hospitality. The following recipe has earned me rave reviews. I have never tasted any poppyseed bread quite like it. If you like cream cheese, you will love it on this bread.

Pre-heat oven to 350 degrees

Grease two loaf pans with cooking spray.

1 box of butter pecan cake mix
1 small package of instant coconut pudding mix
4 eggs
½ c. vegetable oil
1 c. hot water
¼ c. poppy seed

Mix all of the ingredients well with an electric mixer on high speed for 2 minutes. Pour mixture into pans. Bake for 30 minutes. Cool and remove from pans. Slice and serve with softened cream cheese.

Cream Cheese Olive Sandwiches

8 oz. softened cream cheese
½ c. stuffed olives, drained and chopped
2 tbl. mayonnaise

Place all of the above ingredients in a medium size bowl and stir until well blended. Serve with crackers or in phyllo cups. The phyllo cups are found in the frozen foods section at the grocery store. They are great for anything you wish to put in them, especially if you choose not to make your own. The bite size ones are great for tea parties.

A Wedding Buffet

Carving Station

Shrimp and Grits

Green Bean Bundles

Mushroom Fondue

Fruited Pasta Salad

Salmon Spread

Pumpkin Dip

Praline Jam

Green Bean Bundles

3 cans of whole green beans (store brands are good and economical)
8 to 9 slices of bacon cut in half cross-wise
1 8 ounce bottle of Kraft® Catalina dressing

Drain beans. Place a bacon slice on a cutting board. Arrange approximately 10-12 beans in the center and cross-wise of the bacon. Fold bacon over beans from one side, and then lap over from the other side. The bundle should measure the circumference of a small lime.

Place bean bundles on a well-greased 9X13 baking dish. Repeat until bundles have filled the dish and are just touching. Coat the beans evenly with the dressing.

Bake at 300 degrees for 1 1/2 hours. The bacon will be nicely browned on top.

Salmon Spread

For a large party, you may triple or quadruple this recipe. Use a fish mold to give it some interest. Serve on a bed of butter lettuce. Garnish with parsley, using a black olive for the eye.

1 6 oz. pkg. of Red Salmon
2 c. sour cream
1 tsp. lemon juice
2 tbl. fresh parsley, chopped fine
½ tsp. garlic salt
1 tbl. onion flakes

Mix all of the ingredients together until well blended and chill for at' least 2 hours. Serve with crackers or sliced French bread rounds.

Mushroom Fondue

8 slices of day old bread, butter and cubed
1 lb. of sliced mushrooms
8 oz. sharp cheddar cheese
1 c. mayonnaise
1 c. cream of mushroom soup
2 c. milk
1 small onion, chopped fine
½ stick of margarine

Evenly distribute the cubed day old bread in a greased 13 X 9 casserole. Sprinkle grated cheese over the bread cubes. Melt margarine in a large size saucepan on medium heat. Add sliced mushrooms and onions. Sauté until mushrooms are soft and onions are translucent (8-10 minutes). Transfer onions and mushrooms to a medium size mixing bowl. Stir in mushroom soup and mayonnaise until well blended. Slowly pour in the milk stirring until smooth. Blend in salt and pepper. Pour over the bread and cheese mixture. Refrigerate for two hours or overnight. Allow to sit on counter until room temperature – 30 to 45 minutes.

Bake at 350 degrees for 30 minutes or until center is firm.

Fruited Pasta Salad

1 16 oz. box of bowtie pasta
2 cups of honey dew melon or cantaloupe
2 9 oz. boxes of sugar snap peas
1 pint of fresh strawberries, washed and sliced
1 c. poppy seed dressing
1 c. candied nuts of your choice

Cook pasta as directed. Drain and cool. Place pasta in a large salad bowl. Gently stir in dressing to coat the pasta. Set aside. Prepare snap peas as directed, drain and cool for 5 minutes in the refrigerator. Add the peas and melon to the mixture, again stirring gently. Place in the refrigerator a minimum of 1 hour. Just before serving, add sliced strawberries to the salad. Top with nuts.

Pumpkin Dip

I found this recipe in a magazine and used it for both my friend's and my daughter's wedding reception. In the magazine, it was served out of a carved and decorated pumpkin and thus so at both receptions. I have adapted it for a smaller quantity. It is a hit during the holidays.

2 8 oz. packages of cream cheese
3 oz. of canned pumpkin
2/3 cup of sugar
1/2 tsp. pumpkin pie spice

In a large mixing bowl, with a hand mixer beat until smooth. (You will see flecks of the white cream cheese) Serve with thin ginger snaps.

Praline Jam

3 tbl. butter
1 ½ c. brown sugar
¼ c. plain flour
1 ½ c. chopped pecans, toasted
½ c. light corn syrup
4 oz. heavy cream

Evenly place the pecans in a 9 X 9 microwave safe dish. Microwave the pecans on high for 2 minutes. Remove and stir. Place back into the microwave for an additional 2 minutes. Microwaves vary in intensity of temperature. After the first 2 minute interval, microwave for a minute, then taste test. Continue for the additional minute if necessary.

In a separate medium sized microwavable dish, melt the butter on high for 40 to 60 seconds. Remove from microwave. Stir in the sugar, flour and syrup until well blended. Again, return to the microwave and cook on high heat for 2 minutes. Remove and stir. Return to the microwave for 2 additional minutes. Remove and stir in cream and pecans. Sauce will be runny, but will thicken as it cools. Place in a 4 c. glass jar with a lid. Sauce will keep for up to 3 weeks in the refrigerator. Yields about 3 cups.

Serving suggestions:

*Use ½ c. of the sauce to serve over an 8 oz. block of cream cheese. For the wedding, I molded the cream cheese into a heart. Serve with thin ginger snaps.

*For a spicy taste, you may add 1 tsp. of prepared mustard to 1 cup of the sauce and stir well. Pour over an 8 oz. block of cream cheese and serve with captain's wafers.

*You may serve as a topping for ice cream.

Shrimp and Grits

Sauce:

½ stick of butter
¼ c. plain flour
8 oz. fresh mushrooms
2 c. chicken broth
2 c. half and half
2 c. sharp cheddar cheese
¼ c. white wine

Chop mushrooms into small size pieces. In a large skillet, sauté mushrooms in butter on medium high heat, until soft. Reduce heat to medium. Stir in flour with a heat proof spatula. Mixture will be thick and lumpy. Add the chicken broth slowly and continue stirring until the mixture becomes bubbly. Stir in the sharp cheese until smooth. Reduce heat to low and add half and half. Cook on low, gently stirring until mixture just starts to bubble. Add white wine and remove from heat immediately. Cover the sauce with a lid and set aside.

Grits:

Quick cooking grits
½ c. half and half

Cook grits as directed on package to serve eight. Stir in ½ c. half and half, cover and set aside to keep warm. I use a small crock pot on low to keep grits at a perfect temperature. Stir occasionally.

Shrimp:

1 lb. fresh shrimp, peeled and deveined
3 tbl. Butter
Lawry's Seasoned Salt®

Sprinkle shrimp with Lawry's Season salt. Sauté the shrimp in butter on medium high heat, until pink – 3 to 5 minutes or cook on a griddle sprayed with cooking spray. Remove from heat. Stir the shrimp into the sauce.

Spoon grits into individual serving dishes. Add a liberal amount of the shrimp sauce. Top with cheeses, bacon bits and if desired, scallions and/or fresh ground black pepper.

Toppings:

Coarse ground black pepper
Fresh grated black pepper
Fresh grated parmesan cheese
Scallions, chopped

*Serve with toasted French bread and a green salad as a meal.
*Serve buffet style in chafing dishes, toppings separately.
*Serve in martini or shallow wine glasses to compliment the dish as an appetizer.

Christening Day

French Dip au jus

Sautéed Mushrooms

Jean's Twice Baked Potatoes

Avocado Salad

Chocolate Éclair Dessert

Jean's Twice Baked Potatoes

Preheat oven to 400 degrees.

6 medium baked potatoes
2 c. sour cream
½ c. of butter/margarine
½ lb. cooked bacon, drained and chopped or
Commercial bacon bits from the grocery
2 c. sharp cheddar cheese, grated
Salt and pepper to taste

Wash and pierce potatoes with a fork in the center of the longest side of the potato, so that if you sliced the potato in half lengthwise, the fork imprint would be your guide. Do not grease as skins will need to be tough.   Place on oven rack and cook for 1 ½ to 2 hours or until potatoes are soft. Remove from oven. Using paper toweling that has been folded to form a barrier from your hand, slice the hot potatoes lengthwise into two halves. Immediately scoop the pulp of the potato into a mixing bowl, preferably a standing mixer, leaving the shell intact and a thin layer of pulp lining it.   Add the margarine. With a hand mixer, beat the potatoes, and margarine to a smooth consistency.   Add the sour cream and beat again until the consistency is again smooth. Place the shells on a baking sheet and fill with the potato mixture. Sprinkle with grated cheese and then bacon bits. Place in oven and heat for 10 to 15 minutes, or until potatoes are hot through and through.

*These potatoes are great left over and super for breakfast. Just pop them in microwave oven and heat. If you choose, you can freeze the potatoes without toppings. Thaw and heat in a slow oven (300 degrees) until hot through and through, add toppings and place back in oven for 3 to 5 minutes, or until cheese melts.

Sirloin Tip Roast for French Dip Au Jus

A sirloin tip roast yields a generous amount for a large group or may be extended over to the next day for a lovely French dip or for cold roast sandwiches. Recommended size for optimum results and flavor is a 5 to 6 lb. roast.

*Tip: Purchase 10 to 12 lb. roast when on sale and have the butcher cut in half and wrap for freezer.

Place a large roasting pan on stovetop cooking unit. Add just enough oil to coat pan or use cooking spray. On medium high heat, sear roast on both sides, just until brown. Remove pan from heat and sprinkle with garlic powder and pepper on all sides. In a large roasting pan, place a cooking rack in center and transfer the roast to the rack. Be sure to pour any juices from the original pan into the roaster. Place meat thermometer in thickest part of roast. Add one cup of water to bottom of pan. Using aluminum foil, make a tent over the roast. Bake slowly at 300 degrees for 1 ½ to 2 hours, depending on the desired doneness. You will need to check the thermometer every 10 to 15 minutes after about an hour. Using the meat thermometer as your guide, remove the roast when the thermometer registers somewhere in the medium rare zone. The meat will continue to cook after removed from oven, so a medium rare to medium is achieved. Allow the meat to rest for at least 30 minutes before removing foil and making gravy.

Au Jus Gravy

Remove roast and roasting rack from pan. Wrap roast in aluminum foil until ready to slice to seal in juices and heat. Place roasting pan on cooking unit and heat drippings from the roast very slowly. You will need to taste test the drippings for flavor. The amount of drippings will depend on the juices that were released from the roast during the roasting process. If the drippings have a rich flavor and this will depend on the quality of the meat and the amount of marbling throughout the roast, you may need only to thicken the gravy. To thicken, whisk together a ½ cup of water with a heaping tablespoon of plain flour. (Purchased au just gravy mix may be substituted for the flour mixture) Return drippings to medium high heat and pour the flour mixture slowly into the simmering drippings, whisking continuously until desired thickness and lumps are dissolved. If a thicker gravy is desired, repeat process. Kitchen Bouquet® is a great tool for making nice dark brown gravy. Add up to 1 tablespoon or until desired color. Serve gravy over meat or individual ramekins.

Sautéed Mushrooms

1 lb. sliced mushrooms
1 stick margarine
1 c. sherry cooking wine
1 tsp. black pepper
½ tsp. garlic powder (Do not use garlic salt)

In a large saucepan, melt margarine on medium heat. Add the sliced mushrooms and cook for about 15 minutes, or until mushrooms are soft. Add the spices and cooking sherry. Increase heat to high. Cook on high heat stirring often, until there is only a small amount of liquid in saucepan. Reduce heat to simmer and continue to stir occasionally, until ready to serve.

Avocado Salad

1 head of Romaine lettuce, washed and torn into bite size pieces
1 pkg. roasted and sliced almonds
½ c. fresh grated parmesan cheese
2 avocadoes, peeled and sliced into strips
1 pkg. sun dried tomatoes
Kraft® Sun Dried Tomato Vinaigrette Dressing and Marinade

Place sun dried tomatoes in small size mixing bowl. Add ½ c. of the vinaigrette. Allow to marinate for at least 10 minutes or more. Wash and tear the lettuce into bite size pieces, blotting the excess water with paper toweling. Place the lettuce in a salad serving bowl. Add the tomatoes and cheese, tossing to distribute the dressing. Top with avocado slices. Serve with additional dressing on the side.

Chocolate Éclair Dessert

This great dessert is low in fat, especially if you use the low-fat graham crackers, two percent milk and low-fat cool whip. The results are still delicious. I used this for many catering events and it was well received. The guests loved the low fat content with a great taste. I have tasted several versions of the recipe and in my opinion, this one is the best.

2 boxes French vanilla pudding mix
1 8 oz. container of cool whip
2 sleeves of graham crackers
2 ½ c. cold milk

Beat pudding with cold milk as directed on package. Pudding will be softer, due to the additional milk recommended. Add cool whip and blend well.

Spray a 13 X 9 dish with cooking spray, coating both bottom and sides. Layer the bottom on pan with graham crackers making sure that entire bottom is covered. You may need to break a few to cover the casserole. Spoon half of the pudding on the layer of crackers by placing several large spoons of pudding on the crackers and then with a rotating motion, gently spread to prevent crackers from sliding. Add another layer of crackers, and then repeat with the pudding. Add a final layer of crackers to top.

Icing
2 squares (1 oz.) of unsweetened chocolate, melted
2 tbl. corn syrup
1 tsp. vanilla
2 tbl. softened margarine
½ c. sifted confectioners' sugar
4 tbl. milk

Melt the chocolate in a microwave proof medium sized bowl for 30 seconds at a time, stirring between the re-set, until chocolate is smooth. It is easy to burn and you may have to adjust the time, depending on your microwave. When chocolate has melted, add the margarine and then microwave an additional 30 seconds. Stir well, adding corn syrup. When the ingredients have been well blended, stir in the milk. The icing will have a consistency of thick syrup. Add the icing to the top of the layered pudding, again, gently spreading the icing to cover the top. Refrigerate at least 4 to 5 hours, preferably overnight. Cut into squares when serving.

*You will need a glass of water to cleanse your knife, between cuttings. A small spatula is a great tool for removal.

Relish the Holidays

Those distant memories of snaking our way down the hall in reptilian fashion toward Santa's bounty now seems foreign to us. So does the squeals of pleasure from our own children. Now here we are in the land of grandchildren and aren't they grand? Thanksgiving and Christmas brings us all a plethora of joy if we open our hearts to Our Heavenly Father's blessings. As one holiday melts into the next, let us rejoice!

Genesis 9:1 - And God blessed Noah and his sons, and said unto them, Be fruitful and multiply and replenish the earth.

Thanksgiving Feast

Baked Turkey Breast

Cornbread Dressing

Turnip Greens with Roots

Macaroni and Cheese with a Twist

Candied Yams

Rhubarb Salad

Stuffed Celery

Pound Cake

Pecan Pie

Baked Turkey Breast

Preheat oven to 300 degrees.

5 to 6 lb. whole turkey breast, fresh or frozen
2 c. water
2 to 3 ribs celery, washed and cut into 3" pieces
Salt
Black pepper
1 medium onion quartered
¼ c. butter

If using frozen turkey breast, thaw as directed on package. Wash breast in cold water and pat dry with paper toweling. On a cutting board, sprinkle the entire breast, sparingly with garlic salt. Liberally, sprinkle with black pepper. Place the celery and onion in the cavity of the breast, pressing the breast together to secure the vegetables in place. You may use some of the excess skin to help to secure the opening. Carefully place breast on a wire rack and then transfer to roasting pan. Add 2 cups of water. Using heavy duty aluminum foil, make a tent over the bird, sealing edges carefully around the pan. Place in a preheated oven and bake 20 minutes per pound or until the juices run clear. Do not over bake. Remove foil tent and increase heat to 450 degrees. Rub the breast with ¼ cup butter. Return to the oven and cook until golden brown.

*You may place a meat thermometer in the thickest portion of the breast to determine doneness.

Aunt Joanne's Macaroni and Cheese with a Twist

8 oz. box of elbow macaroni, cooked and drained
8 oz. sharp cheddar cheese, grated
1 8 oz. jar of chopped pimento, drained
1 large jar of mushroom bits and pieces, drained well
1 medium onion, chopped fine
1 c. mayonnaise
1 can of cream of mushroom soup
1 sleeve of buttery crackers, crushed
4 tbl. margarine, melted

Cook and drain macaroni as directed on package.

In a large mixing bowl combine the next 6 ingredients and stir until smooth. Stir in the macaroni and mix well with a spatula. Pour mixture into a greased 13 X 9 casserole dish. Combine crumbs with melted butter. Add to the top of the macaroni and cheese. Bake on 350 degrees until bubbly.

Stuffed Celery

This recipe is a refreshing change from the pimento cheese stuffed celery traditionally prepared at Thanksgiving.

16 oz. softened cream cheese
½ c. stuffed olives, drained and coarsely chopped
1 c. sharp grated cheese or ½ c. crumbled blue cheese, optional
4 tbl. mayonnaise

Mix all ingredients in a medium size bowl until well blended.

Cut 1 to 2 stalks of washed and trimmed celery hearts into 3 to 4 inch pieces. Fill each celery boat with the cream cheese spread. Place on a serving platter.

Two versions of cornbread dressing are included, the first being from Mary Frances. Hers is light and dipped with a serving spoon. Dorrie's is a firmer texture and can be cut into squares. Both are delicious and are simply a matter of personal preference. You will not be disappointed by choosing either one.

Frances' Cornbread Dressing

1 recipe of egg bread
8 hamburger buns, toasted lightly
6 c. roaster/hen broth
6 eggs
2 tsp. black pepper
1 tsp. salt
2 c. diced celery hearts
4 c. sweet onions, diced
1 to ½ c. water
2 tbl. baking powder

Prepare egg bread as directed below:

5 eggs
1 stick of margarine
1 3/4 cup corn meal mix
1 cup buttermilk

Pre-heat oven to 400 degrees
Melt butter in a medium sized microwave safe bowl for 1 minute. Remove from microware. Whisk in the buttermilk until thoroughly blended to cool the mixture. Add the eggs and whisk again until well blended. Add corn meal and stir thoroughly. Pour batter into a greased 9" iron skillet that has been heated in oven for 7 minutes. Bake for 25 to 30 minutes, or until golden brown.

Prepare day old hamburger buns as directed below:
Preheat oven to 300 degrees. Place bun tops and bottoms in a single layer on a large jelly roll style pan. Bake for 20 to 25 minutes until

lightly browned. Set aside. Do not allow to get too brown.

Wash and place a 5 to 7 lb. roaster or hen in a large stock pot with just enough water to cover the top of the bird. Bring to a boil over high heat. Reduce heat to simmer, cover and simmer for 2 hours.

Place the diced celery and onion in a medium saucepan and cover with just enough water to cover the vegetables. Bring to a boil on high heat, reduce heat to low and cook for about 10 minutes. Remove from heat. In an extra large mixing bowl, crumble the egg bread and the buns into pieces no larger than a marble. Sprinkle with seasonings and stir well. Stir in the cooked celery and onion, and the chicken broth. (Freeze any remaining broth for later use) Beat the eggs together in a medium sized mixing bowl with a wire whisk. Add to the dressing mixture, stirring until well blended. Grease two 9 X 13 casserole dishes with cooking spray. Pour half the dressing into one of the casserole dishes and the other half into the remaining dish.

Bake in pre-heated oven for 30 to 40 minutes or until center is firm.

Dorrie's Cornbread Dressing

1 recipe of egg bread
1 recipe of biscuits
6 c. roaster/hen broth
6 eggs
2 tsp. black pepper
1 tsp. salt
2 c. diced celery hearts
2 medium size sweet onions, diced
2 tsp. dried sage
1 c. buttermilk, stir in a pinch of soda

Step 1: Prepare egg bread as directed below:
2 eggs
1 stick of margarine
1 3/4 cup of corn meal mix
1 cup or buttermilk

Melt butter in a medium sized microwave safe bowl for 1 minute. Remove from microware. Whisk in the buttermilk. Add the eggs and whisk until well blended. Stir in the cornmeal. Pour into greased 9" iron skillet that has been heated in oven for 5 to 7 minutes. Bake at 400 degrees for 25 to 30 minutes, or until golden brown.

Step 2: Prepare dozen biscuits as directed below:
½ stick of shortening
2 c. self- rising flour
1c. whole buttermilk

Place the flour in a medium sized mixing bowl. Cut the shortening in with a pastry knife or use gloved hand, until the shortening has been distributed throughout and pieces are the size of a dime. Add the buttermilk and gently blend with spoon or hand, until all flour has been incorporated and forms a soft dough. Overworking the dough can make the biscuits tough. Handle dough as little as possible. With floured hands, pinch off dough in golf ball sizes and roll in floured palms until smooth. Place biscuits on greased baking pan and pat with fingers to make a ½ inch thick biscuit. Repeat process, placing the biscuits on the baking pan, so that they touch. Bake at 400 degrees until golden brown, about 15 to 20 minutes.

*If desired, place the dough on a floured pastry sheet and roll the dough out with a floured rolling pin making a large circle 12 inches in diameter and about 1 inch in thickness. Use a biscuit cutter to cut 12 biscuits. You may need to reshape the dough into a ball and roll out again to make the dozen biscuits.

Step 3:
Wash and place a 5 to 7 lb. roaster or hen in a large stock pot with just enough water to cover the top of the bird. Bring to a boil over high heat. Reduce heat to simmer, cover and cook for 2 hours.

Step 4:
Place the diced celery and onion in a medium saucepan and cover with just enough water to cover the vegetables. Bring to a boil on high heat, reduce heat to low and cook for about 10 minutes. Remove from heat. In an extra large mixing bowl, crumble the egg bread and the biscuits into pieces no large than a marble. Place on a large baking sheet and place in a 300 degree oven, until breads are lightly toasted, about 15 to 20 minutes. Remove from oven and return to large bowl. Sprinkle with seasonings and stir well. Stir in the cooked celery and onion, and the chicken broth. Beat the eggs together in a medium sized mixing bowl with a wire whisk. Add buttermilk and eggs to the dressing mixture, stirring until well blended. Grease two a 9 X 13 casserole dishes with cooking spray. Pour half the dressing into one of the casserole dishes and the other half into the remaining dish. Bake at 400 degrees until center of dressing is firm, about 45 minutes to 50 minutes.

*For a special treat for the adults in the family, stir in 1 tsp. of red pepper flakes in the second half of dressing, before baking. Just thinking about that extra kick that the red pepper flakes add to this holiday favorite leaves many of us in our family wishing the holidays would never end. As the men in my family lament – sweet!

Rhubarb Salad

This recipe was used one Christmas when mother's oven was not working. She wanted to find something that was colorful and would serve as a holiday dessert.

2 c. diced red apples
1 small envelope of strawberry Jell-O®
8 oz. frozen rhubarb
1 c. of frozen strawberries, sweetened
1 c. water
1 c. pineapple juice
1 c. chopped nuts
1 c. of sour cream
10 to 12 whole strawberries for garnish

Cook rhubarb in 1 c. of water until tender, about 15 minutes. Stir in the gelatin until dissolved. Add the pineapple juice and continue stirring until well blended. Stir in the strawberries, nuts and apples. Pour into a 13 X 9 casserole dish. Refrigerate until gelatin is firm, about two hours. Garnish with a layer of the sour cream and whole strawberries. Cut into squares and serve.

In a medium size mixing bowl, cream butter and sugar with an electric mixer. Add corn syrup and blend well, then add eggs one at a time, beating well after each addition. Stir in nuts, vanilla and salt. Spoon mixture into pie shells. Bake for 50 minutes or until a toothpick comes out clean when inserted into the center.

Turnip Greens with Roots

1 lb. package washed turnip greens
4 medium size roots, washed and peeled
1 ham hock
2 qts. of water
½ tsp. salt
½ tsp. pepper

Wash the meat and place in 2 quarts of water in a medium stock pot and bring to a boil over high heat. Add the greens and bring back to a boil. Cover and reduce heat to low. Cook for 1 hour and then add the roots to the top of greens. Add salt and pepper. Cook and additional 30 to 40 minutes or until roots are fork tender. Remove greens and roots from the pot with a slotted spoon, reserving the pot licker. Chop with a hand chopper until well mixed and roots are chopped fine, adding pot licker as needed to achieve the desired consistency. Remove the ham from the ham bone and tear into strings and chop into greens. Serve with cornbread.

*Greens freeze well. Thaw in warm water and heat in a lightly oiled skillet on medium high heat, stirring often until thoroughly heated.

Candied Yams

3 to 4 lbs. of medium sweet potatoes
(Choose potatoes that have skin that is reddish orange in color)
Mazola oil or peanut oil, your preference
1 to 2 sticks of margarine
1 c. granulated sugar

Place potatoes in very hot tap water to loosen the skin and make for easier peeling. Peel the potatoes. Cut into wedges of different sizes, down the length of the potato, making sure that the potatoes are a little less than a half inch thick, and not longer than about four inches. Do not cut the potatoes in a uniform fashion. The secret to their flavor lies in the shape of the potatoes. I have tried cutting them into round slices and the results are not the same.

You may deep fry or fry potatoes in an iron Dutch oven in about an inch of oil. Any Dutch oven will work. Bring the oil to medium high heat and add potatoes in a single layer, turning quickly, as they will brown very fast. Make sure the potatoes are light to dark brown, before removing them individually, then adding another batch of potatoes to the oil before it becomes too hot. Additional oil may be required, as the potatoes do absorb some of it. If you add more, make sure the temperature reaches a medium high before adding more potatoes. Occasionally, the oil will begin to get too hot and start smoking, remove from the heat. Continue the frying process until all of the potatoes are browned.

Once all of the potatoes have been fried, discard the oil, and add one stick of margarine to the Dutch oven. Place the potatoes back in it and sprinkle evenly with one cup of sugar. Cover and reduce heat to low immediately. Simmer for about 15 to 20 minutes, or until a syrup is formed. Do not stir the potatoes. Gently shift them with a spatula, so that they are covered in the syrup. Taste the potatoes and sweeten to your satisfaction, (You may add additional butter and sugar, reducing the butter and sugar to half of the original proportions, i.e., ½ stick of margarine and ½ cup of sugar.) Heat on low with the lid on. The sugar will melt into a syrup.

Pound Cake

Preheat oven to 325 degrees. Grease and lightly flour a tube pan, set aside.

1 lb. sugar (2 2/3 c.)
8 eggs, room temperature
1 lb. cake flour (3 ½ c. sifted, plain)
1 lb. butter, lightly salted
8 tbl. whipping cream or canned milk
1 tsp. vanilla

Separate eggs and whip whites until they are stiff, adding 6 tbl. of sugar while beating. Refrigerate immediately. Cream butter on medium high speed of mixer, adding the sugar gradually and beating until light and fluffy. Add egg yolks two at a time, beating well after each addition. Then, add vanilla, beating just until mixed. Add the flour and cream alternately, beginning and ending with the flour and beating well after each addition. Then beat on low speed of mixer for 10 minutes. Fold in egg whites gently, until mixture is well blended. Pour batter into tube pan, scraping down sides of bowl with a rubber spatula. Smooth top of batter with the spatula and gently tap pan on kitchen counter to distribute batter evenly. Bake for one hour and fifteen minutes or until a toothpick comes out clean when inserted into the center of cake. Allow to cool for about 10 minutes. With a dull knife, loosen the cake from the pan, by running the knife around the outside edge and the center edge of pan. Turn onto a plate, and then gently place a cake serving plate on top and invert, so that the cake rests on the cake serving plate.

*If you choose, spread with your favorite icing.

Pecan Pie

Pre-heat oven to 350 degrees.

3 c. whole pecans
1 c. corn syrup
1 c. light brown sugar
6 eggs
½ tsp. salt
1 stick of butter
3 unbaked pie shells (Do not use deep dish)

In a medium size mixing bowl, cream butter and sugar with an electric mixer. Add corn syrup and blend well, then add eggs one at a time, beating well after each addition. Stir in nuts and salt. Spoon mixture into pie shells. Bake for 50 minutes or until a toothpick comes out clean when inserted into the center.

T

Thanksgiving Remnants

Turkey Cranberry Sandwiches

Curry Sauce

Plum Sauce

Turkey Cranberry Sandwiches

1 lb. roasted turkey breast
4 slices of Muenster cheese
Green leaf lettuce
1 s. can whole berry cranberry sauce
4 oz. cream cheese
2 tbl. Orange marmalade
9 grain bread, sliced

Wash the lettuce leaves and pat dry with paper toweling. In a small mixing bowl, mix the cream cheese with orange marmalade until well blended.

Spread about 2 tbls. of the cream cheese mixture on one side of four slices of bread. Spread about 2 tbls. of the whole cranberry sauce on four additional slices of bread.

To assemble sandwiches:

Layer the turkey equally on the bread slices that has been spread with the cream cheese mixture.
Add cheese slices, then lettuce leaves
Top each sandwich with the remaining bread slices that have been spread with the cranberry sauce

Sauces can be added or exchanged to your liking for your leftover turkey. Prepare sauces a day ahead and set up a sandwich bar for lingering guests or for a quick and easy supper. Add store bought chips, pickles and relishes, if desired.

Curry Sauce

1 c. sour cream
½ c. mayonnaise
3 tbl. lemon juice
2 tbl. minced onion
2 tbl. minced parsley, fresh
1 tbl. curry powder, or up to 2 tbl. to taste
1 tbl. mustard
Dash of paprika
2 drops of Tabasco

Mix together in a medium bowl with an airtight lid. Makes two cups and can be kept for several days. Great with seafood, fish, pork or turkey.

Plum Sauce

This recipe is a repeat from the wedding menu and is equally good on pork, beef or chicken.

1 c. red plum jam
1 tbl. prepared horseradish
1 tbl. prepared mustard
1 tsp. lemon juice

Combine the above ingredients in a small saucepan and cook over medium heat until bubbly. Yields 1 cup.

Welcome Christmas Morning!

Applewood Smoked Bacon and
Cheese Fondue or

Scalloped Oysters

Baked Apples

Cream Cheese Cinnamon Danish

Assorted Breads

Wassail

Scalloped Oysters

Preheat oven to 400 degrees.

8 tbl. butter
1 medium onion, minced
½ rib of celery with leaves, minced
2 c. fine dry bread or cracker crumbs
½ c. chopped parsley
2 pints of shucked oysters, with liquor
1 c. heavy cream
2 tsp. Worcestershire sauce
½ tsp. salt
½ tsp. hot pepper sauce
Paprika

Melt butter in a medium skillet over medium heat. Sauté onion and celery until golden. Add crumbs and sauté again, until the crumbs begin to brown, mixture will be dry. Stir in parsley and transfer to a bowl.

Drain oysters, reserving liquid. Set oysters aside. Place liquid into the skillet. Add cream, Worcestershire sauce, salt and hot pepper sauce, mixing well. Simmer, stirring often until mixture is slightly thickened, about 5 to 7 minutes.

Place about one third of the oysters in a well-greased 9 X 13 baking dish. Cover evenly with about a third of the crumb mixture, repeating with two more layers ending with the crumb mixture. Pour cream sauce over the layers. Sprinkle with paprika. Bake until bubbly and brown, about 25 to 30 minutes.

Cheese Fondue

Pre-heat oven to 350 degrees

3 slices of day old bread
½ stick margarine, softened
2 c. milk
3 eggs
½ tsp. salt
2 c. sharp cheese, grated

Spread bread slices with softened margarine and cut in 1½ inch cubes. Grease a 9 X 13 casserole dish with cooking spray. Arrange bread in the bottom of the casserole with the buttered side up. In a medium size mixing bowl, beat eggs with a wire whisk. Add milk, salt and continue to whisk together until well blended. Sprinkle the cheese evenly over the cubed bread. Pour the milk mixture over the bread and cheese. Let stand in the refrigerator a minimum of 30 minutes or overnight. Remove from the refrigerator and bake on the top rack of the oven for 25 to 30 minutes. Top will be lightly brown. Insert a toothpick into the center of cheese fondue and when removed, it should come out clean.

Wassail

Not only does this drink taste wonderful, it will smell heavenly as it steeps, especially during the holidays.

½ gallon apple cider
1 ½ quart cranberry juice cocktail
¼ c. brown sugar
4 sticks cinnamon
2 tsp. cloves

Combine ingredients in a 4 qt. stockpot. Bring to a boil over medium high heat. Reduce heat and simmer for 20 minutes, then remove cloves. Serve warm.

Baked Apples

4 Granny Smith Apples
4 tbl. light brown sugar, firmly packed
4 tbl. butter or margarine
4 tbl. chopped walnuts
2 c. water
Cinnamon

Preheat oven to 350 degrees.

Grease a 9X9 casserole with cooking spray; add the water to the bottom of the pan.

Wash and core apples being careful not to pierce the bottom. Place 1 tbl. of butter or margarine in center of each apple. Top with 1 tbl. firmly packed brown sugar and 1 tbl. of chopped walnuts. Sprinkle apples liberally with cinnamon. Place in the casserole. Cover with foil and bake 45 minutes or until the apples are soft. Remove foil and cook an additional 15 minutes. The liquid will form a syrup. Spoon syrup over apples when served.

Jenny's Cream Cheese Cinnamon Danish

2 cans of crescent rolls
2 8 oz. packages of cream cheese
1 C. sugar
1 egg white, lightly beaten until foamy

Topping

½ c. sugar
1 tsp. cinnamon

Preheat oven to 350 degrees.

Grease a 9X13 casserole dish. Spread one can of the rolls on the bottom of casserole dish, pressing the triangle shaped dough to form a square, then connecting all to form a crust.

Cream the sugar and cream cheese together with an electric mixer, in a medium size mixing bowl. Spread gently on the crust, being careful to keep crust intact. Repeat the process of making a crust for the top of the Danish as instructed above. Spread the egg whites evenly over the crust. Sprinkle the cinnamon topping evenly over the crust and bake for 30 minutes. Allow to cool before cutting into squares.

Relish the Wait...

Seasonal Offerings

Wonderful Winter

Pork Roast and Gravy

Steamed White Rice

English Peas

Mock Pecan Pie

Pork Roast and Gravy

3 to 5 lb. pork loin roast
2 tbl. Cooking oil
½ c. water
Salt and pepper
1 Tbl. *Kitchen Bouquet®*

Thickener for gravy
¼ c. flour
½ c. water

Pour cooking oil in a Dutch oven. On medium high heat, lightly brown roast on all sides. Salt and pepper roast on all sides, ending with fat side up. Add ½ c. water, reduce heat to low and cover. Cook for 1½ to 2 hours or until thermometer registers 180 degrees when inserted into the center of meat.

To make gravy, stir in the Kitchen Bouquet® into the drippings from the pork with a wire whisk until evenly distributed, and spoon over the roast. In a small bowl, whisk together flour and water until smooth. Add the flour mixture slowly into the drippings, stirring constantly to thicken gravy. Remove roast from Dutch oven. Slice into ½ inch slices and place on a platter. Spoon small amount of gravy over roast slices and garnish with parsley.

*Note: Liquid from roast may vary. Additional thickening mixture may be made and added in small increments, stirring constantly to desired consistency of gravy.

English Peas

1 ½ c. fresh or frozen English peas
1 medium ham hock
1 qt. of water
½ c. milk
2 eggs, boiled and diced
½ tsp. salt
½ tsp. pepper

Rinse meat and place in water in a medium stock pot. Bring to a boil over high heat. Add the peas and bring back to a boil. Cover and reduce heat to low. Cook for 1 hour for frozen peas or 1 hour 15 minutes for fresh peas, or until peas are fork tender. Add salt and pepper, stirring gently to blend spices, and then add milk and eggs. Cover and extinguish heat. Allow to sit for at least 15 to 20 minutes or until ready to serve.

*Re-heat on medium low.

Mock Pecan Pie

3 egg whites
1 c. sugar
1 tsp. baking powder
1 tsp. vanilla
16 Ritz® crackers (crumbled - not crushed)
1/2 to 1 cup of pecans (I use 1 cup)

Place the first 4 ingredients in a 2 quart mixing bowl. Beat until the consistency of a meringue, thick and fluffy but not firm. Fold in pecans and crackers. Bake in a greased pie pan 30-35 minutes at 300 degrees until light brown.

Cheese Biscuits

Pre-heat oven to 400 degrees

½ c. of margarine, cold
2 c. self-rising flour
1 c. whole buttermilk
8 oz. sharp cheddar cheese, grated

Place the flour in a medium sized mixing bowl. Cut the margarine in with a pastry cutter or use gloved hand, until the margarine has been distributed throughout and pieces are the size of a dime. Add the buttermilk and gently blend with spoon or hand, until all the flour has been incorporated and dough is formed. (Working too much flour into the dough can make biscuits too heavy.) Add the cheese and blend well until evenly distributed into dough. With floured hands, pinch off dough in golf ball sizes and roll in floured palms until smooth. Place biscuits on greased baking pan and pat with fingers to make a ½ inch thick biscuit. Repeat process, placing the biscuits on the pan, so that they touch. Allow biscuits sit on counter for about 30 minutes, if time allows, for a nice smooth appearance when baked. Yields 14 to 16 biscuits.

Spring Reflections

Dorrie's Baked Chicken and Gravy

Potato Salad

Country Style Green Beans

Dorrie's Cornbread Muffins

Layer Cake with

Old Fashioned Chocolate Icing

Dorrie's Corn Bread Muffins

I am lucky enough to have an iron muffin tin that my mother found in an antique store. Each one of the sections has a cone like shape that flares at the top, creating a scalloped edge on the baked muffin, which is oh so crunchy! If you are lucky enough to find one, it is worth its weight in gold! It will last forever and will be an heirloom to be handed down for generations. They are rare. I own three, two of which make half of a dozen muffins. You may certainly use the traditional muffin tin and will have great success.

If you choose to use the batter for corn bread to be sliced, use a 9 inch pan. It is best when made in an iron skillet that has been greased and heated in the oven while preparing the batter. Be careful not to overheat the pan or muffin tin. About 5 to 7 minutes should prepare the pan/tin nicely. The recipe below yields 6 to 8 servings of corn bread or 12 corn muffins.

Pre-heat oven to 400 degrees

1 egg
1 stick of margarine
1 ¼ cup of corn meal mix
1 cup of whole buttermilk

Melt butter in a medium sized microwave safe bowl for 1 minute. Remove from microware. Whisk in the buttermilk, until thoroughly blended to cool the mixture. Then, add the egg and whisk thoroughly. Stir in the cornmeal mix until well blended. Pour into greased corn muffin tin to yield 12 equal sized muffins or a greased 12 inch iron skillet. Bake for 15 to 20 minutes, or until golden brown.

*You may fill the buttermilk into the measuring cup to almost full, topping off with about 1/8 of a cup of water to make the corn muffins crunchier.

Dorrie's Baked Chicken and Gravy

1 large roaster (3-5 lbs.)
1 large sweet onion
2 stalks of celery
2 tbls. margarine
Salt
Black Pepper

Wash chicken thoroughly. Drain water from cavity of the bird. Place bird on a prep surface. Cut both ends of onion and peel thin layer of skin away. Cut onion in half horizontally and then quarter each half. Wash and cut two stalks of celery into 2 to 3 inch pieces. Place the bird on the backside. Stuff the onions and celery into the bird's cavity, placing half of the onion and half the celery first, and then finish by alternating the vegetables, discarding vegetables that will not fit inside bird. Most birds will have some excess skin that will help to contain the vegetables, by pulling the skin across the opening of the cavity. You may also use poultry string to tie the legs together if you choose. Lightly salt and pepper the outside skin of the bird. Place the bird in a covered Dutch oven. Bake in a 300 degree oven for two hours. Remove lid and baste with melted butter. Return to oven and increase temperature to 400 degrees to bring bird to a golden brown. This should take around 10 minutes. I use an iron Dutch oven and often the bird will have browned in the first two hours. Carefully remove from oven, using a spatula to loosen underside of bird, removing any skin that may have adhered to the bottom of oven. Place on platter. Make gravy with remaining broth.

Chicken Gravy

1 cup drippings and broth from baked chicken
2 tbl. of self-rising corn meal mix
2 cups of water

Use a spatula to scrape the broth and drippings from the bottom of the Dutch oven. Pour the drippings in a small mixing bowl, place in the freezer and leave until fat from the bird coagulates. (30 minutes or so) Remove from freezer, skim off fat, and measure remainder of broth to one full cup. Add back some of the fat, if necessary, to fill measuring cup.

In a small bowl, whisk together corn meal with 1 cup of the water. Place broth back in Dutch oven; bring to boil on high heat. Reduce heat to low. Add corn meal mixture slowly to the broth, using whisk to incorporate the two. As mixture thickens, slowly add the other cup of water, using whisk to stir constantly. Increase heat to medium high, stirring until the gravy is bubbly. Cover and extinguish heat, until ready to serve.

Serve over Corn Bread or Corn Muffins.

Potato Salad

2 ½ lbs. of Idaho potatoes, peeled and cubed
3 eggs, boiled
1 ½ ribs of celery hearts, diced thin
½ c. sweet pickle relish, drained
¾ c. sharp cheddar cheese
½ c. mayonnaise
¼ tsp. salt
¼ tsp. Lawry's Seasoned Salt®
1 tsp. black pepper

In a medium saucepan, place eggs and cover with water. Bring to a boil over high heat. Cover and reduce heat to low and cook an additional 15 minutes on low. Remove from heat and allow to col.

In a large stock pot, add cubed potatoes and add enough water to just cover them. Bring to a boil over high heat. Cover and reduce heat to low and cook until potatoes are fork tender, about 20 minutes. Drain potatoes and place on a cookie sheet. Sprinkle with seasonings. Place in refrigerator and allow to cool.

In a large mixing bowl, place eggs, cheese, celery and pickles. Chop with the blade of a hand chopper into small cubes. With a rubber spatula, add mayonnaise and stir until smooth.

Remove the potatoes from the refrigerator. Fold the cooled potatoes in to the egg mixture, stirring gently and adding additional mayonnaise, if desired. Cover and allow to cool in refrigerate for at least 2 hours. You may garnish with bacon bits, parsley, pimento or nothing at all. The longer the salad "rests" the better the flavor!

Dorrie's 1 -2- 3 -4 Cake Layers

A surprising twist to the standard 1- 2- 3- 4 cake layers is the incorporation of buttermilk, replacing sweet milk, making the layers light and fluffy. Once, mother had to make four cakes for a fundraiser to support our basketball team. Since Jan and I were on the same team, we had to provide two each. She iced each one differently. Her cakes were a great hit.

Pre-heat oven to 350 degrees

1 c. butter or shortening
2 c. sugar
3 c. cake flour
4 eggs
1 c. buttermilk
3 tsp. baking powder
½ tsp. salt
1 tsp. vanilla

Sift the dry ingredients together. Set aside. Cream butter or shortening and sugar in a large mixing bowl with an electric mixer until fluffy. Add eggs one at a time, beating well after each addition. Add the dry ingredients in fourths to the creamed mixture, alternately with the buttermilk in thirds, beginning and ending with the dry ingredients. Do not over-beat, but make sure to incorporate well, after each addition. Stir in vanilla. Grease and lightly flour three cake pans and divide batter in the pans. Bake for 25 to 30 minutes until the center springs back when lightly touched. Remove from oven to cooling rack. Cool on racks for 10 minutes. Release from edge of pans with a dull knife and turn onto parchment paper. Allow layers to cool, and spread the cake layers with your favorite icing or frosting, stacking and frosting top and sides. Old fashioned chocolate icing follows.

Old Fashioned Chocolate Icing

MaMa made a chocolate cake that earned her the respect of many in her community. I use mother's cake layer recipe above and then ice with MaMa's chocolate icing recipe. Also, I halve each layer, using a serrated knife, once the layers are completely cool to create 6 thin layers. This means more chocolate and perfect satisfaction. One trick that MaMa used was to leave the baking powder out of the batter and cook 5 to 6 thin layers. Yummy! None the less, whatever you choose to use this icing on, you will not regret it.

2 c. sugar
½ c. cocoa
½ c. butter or margarine
½ c. milk
2 tsp. vanilla

Mix sugar and cocoa in a medium size saucepan with a wooden spoon. Add butter or margarine and milk. Cook and stir over medium high heat until the mixture comes to a rolling boil. Remove from heat and allow the mixture to cool. Add vanilla and beat until creamy and consistency to spread.

Country Style Green Beans

2 lbs. green beans
3 slices of pre-cut salt pork
1 qt. of water
1 tsp. salt
1 tsp. pepper

Snap fresh beans into 3" pieces and wash with cold water in a colander. Place meat and water in a large stock pot and bring to a boil over high heat. Add the green beans and bring back to a boil. Cover and reduce heat to low. Cook for 2 hours. Remove lid and turn on medium high heat. Add salt and pepper, stirring gently to blend spices. Cook until all of the water has been absorbed, checking often so that the beans do not stick. You may turn heat to low when about a 1/4 c. of water on bottom of stock pot remains, again checking often. Do not stir beans, gently use spoon to check water level. When all water has all been absorbed, remove immediately from heat and cover until ready to serve.

My Favorite Please!

Jan's Fried Chicken Fingers

Macaroni and Cheese

Lady Peas

Jalapeno Corn Bread

Deviled Eggs

Turtle Brownies

Jan's Fried Chicken Fingers

4 boneless skinless chicken breasts
2 c. buttermilk
3 c. self-rising flour
1 tbl. Lawry's Seasoned Salt®
1 tbl. black pepper
4 c. peanut oil

Wash chicken thoroughly in cold water and drain well, pat dry with paper toweling. On a cutting surface, cut each breast into 4 strips. Place strips in a plastic gallon bag and add buttermilk. Seal and place in in refrigerator overnight. Remove chicken from refrigerator. Place the flour in another gallon bag and add seasoned salt and black pepper. Shake to distribute the seasonings. Remove half the fingers from the buttermilk and place into the flour mixture. Seal and shake to coat the fingers. After coating with flour mixture, place fingers on paper toweling. Repeat process with the remaining chicken fingers.

Heat the oil in a fryer or in a cast iron skillet, on medium high heat. Sprinkle a pinch of flour into the hot oil to test if it sizzles. Slowly drop about half the fingers into the oil, allowing the oil to begin bubbling around each finger, before adding additional fingers. Remove individually from the grease with a slotted spoon when golden brown. Working quickly, add the remainder of the fingers and cook as instructed above until golden brown.

Macaroni and Cheese

I have recently adapted my recipe at my family's request to add some different cheeses. They have been very pleased. Once you master the sauce, you may substitute the cheese or cheeses of your choice, using the same increments as the recipe suggests. If you like browned macaroni and cheese, bake in a metal pan.

1 8 oz. box of elbow macaroni
5 oz. Kraft Cracker Barrel Sharp Cheddar Cheese®, grated
5 oz. Kraft Monterrey and Colby Jack Cheese Blend®, grated
2 c. of half and half
½ tsp. salt
1 dash of Worcestershire sauce
¼ tsp. dried mustard
2 heaping tbl. self-rising flour
4 tbl. margarine

Cook macaroni as directed on package and drain. Place in a large mixing bowl and set aside. In a medium sized saucepan, melt margarine over medium heat, stirring constantly. Immediately stir in the flour, continuing to stir until well blended, making a roué. Remove from heat and stir in dried mustard, Worcestershire sauce and salt. Return to heat and slowly stir the half and half into the mixture, using a wire whisk. Continue to whisk, increasing the heat to medium high, until thick and bubbly. Immediately remove from heat and add grated cheese, stirring until melted. The sauce will become thick. Pour cheese sauce over the macaroni and gently blend with a spatula. Grease a 9 X 13 casserole dish with cooking spray. Pour the macaroni and cheese sauce evenly in the casserole dish. Bake at 350 degrees for 25 to 30 minutes until lightly brown on top. You may add buttered bread cubes as a topping if desired or additional grated cheese.

Lady Peas

1 ½ c. fresh/frozen Lady Peas or peas of your choice
2 slices of pre-cut salt pork
1 qt. of water
½ tsp. salt
½ tsp. pepper

Place meat and water in a medium stock pot and bring to a boil over high heat. Add the peas and bring back to a boil. Cover and reduce heat to low. Cook for 1 hour for frozen peas or 1 hour 15 minutes for fresh or until peas are fork tender. Add salt and pepper, stirring gently to blend spices, cover and extinguish heat. Allow to sit until ready to serve.

Re-heat on medium low if desired.

Deviled Eggs

6 eggs, hard boiled
1/3 c. sweet pickle relish
2 tbl. mayonnaise
Finely ground black pepper
Salt
Paprika

Place 6 eggs in a small saucepan and cover with COLD water. Bring to a boil over high heat. Cover and extinguish heat. Allow to sit for 15 minutes. Remove and run cool water over eggs. Peel and slice in half lengthwise. Remove yolks and place in a shallow dish. Place halves in an egg dish and set aside. Cream together egg yolks and mayonnaise with a fork. Add pickles and mix until smooth. Add salt and pepper to taste. Stuff creamed mixture into eggs with a spoon. Sprinkle lightly with paprika.

Jalapeno Corn Bread

The jalapeno peppers in this recipe may be just a slight bit spicy, but the ingredients make this recipe masterful – a wedge will make you wonder if the bread is not the main course.

1 ¾ c. self-rising corn meal mix
1 c. grated sharp cheddar cheese
1 c. buttermilk
2/3 c. cooking oil
2 eggs, beaten
1 c. onion, finely chopped
1 to 3 Jalapeno peppers, seed removed and diced
1 12 oz. can cream style corn

Pre-heat oven to 300 degrees

Grease a 12 inch iron skillet or aluminum pan with cooking spray. Mix all the ingredients together in a medium size mixing bowl. Place iron skillet in a preheated oven for about 5 minutes. Remove from oven and pour batter into pan. Cook for 1 hour to 1 hour fifteen minutes or until golden brown. Allow bread to cool for at least 15 minutes before cutting into wedges. Bread will be moist and can be eaten with a fork. As the bread cools, the texture will firm up, but will remain very moist.

*A 9 X 13 baking dish or aluminum pan may be used and will not require heating once sprayed with oil. Leftover cornbread is wonderful heated slowly in a 250 to 300 degree oven.

**Jalapeno Cornbread Croutons - You may slice leftover cornbread into 1 inch slices, then cut in half and further into cubes. Heat in a 250 to 300 degree oven until toasted. Serve as croutons on salads, YUM!

Turtle Brownies

Pre-heat oven to 350 degrees

1 box German chocolate cake mix
1 c. evaporated milk
¾ c. butter flavored shortening
1 10 oz. bag of Kraft® caramels
1 c. chopped nuts
1 8 oz. bag of Toll House® morsels

Grease a 10 X 13 X ¾ cookie sheet.

Using an electric hand mixer, combine the cake mix, ½ c. of the evaporated milk and shortening in a medium sized mixing bowl, on medium speed of mixer for 1 to 2 minutes. Spread half of the cake mix in the bottom of the cookie sheet. Bake at 350 degrees for 8 minutes. Remove paper from the caramels and place in a microwave safe dish, along with the remainder of the milk. Microwave in 1 minute intervals, stirring after each interval, until caramel is smooth. Pour over the cake. Sprinkle with the chocolate morsels and nuts. Spoon remaining cake mix over the top, using the back of a wet spoon to smooth the batter evenly over the layers. Bake for 22 minutes at 350 degrees. Remove from oven and allow to cool completely. Cut into squares.

A Gentle Hug

Jenifer's Meatloaf

Creamy Mashed Potatoes

Petite Lima Beans

Yeast Muffin Surprise

Cheesy Apples

Jefiner's Meatloaf

Preheat oven to 350 degrees.

1 lb. lean ground beef
2 slices bread, slowly toasted
¼ tsp. garlic powder
½ tsp. salt
½ tsp. black pepper
Dash of Worcestershire sauce
1 lb. can of tomatoes, pureed
¼ c. green pepper, chopped fine
¼ c. onion, chopped fine
¼ c. celery, chopped fine

Topping:
½ c. Ketchup
1 tbl. light brown sugar
1 tbl. lemon juice

Combine all of the above ingredients in a large bowl. Place in a greased loaf pan and bake for 1 hour on 350 degrees. In a small mixing bowl, blend ketchup, brown sugar and lemon juice with a wire whisk. Using a rubber spatula, coat top of meatloaf with the sauce the last 15 minutes of cook time.

Petite Lima Beans

1 ½ c. fresh green butterbeans
2 slices of pre-cut salt pork
1 qt. of water
½ tsp. salt
½ tsp. pepper

Place meat and water in a medium stock pot and bring to a boil over high heat. Add the peas and bring back to a boil. Cover and reduce heat to low. Cook for 1 hour for frozen peas or 1 hour 15 minutes for fresh or until peas are fork tender. Add salt and pepper, stirring gently to blend spices, cover and extinguish heat. Allow to sit until ready to serve.

Re-heat on medium low if desired.

Cheesy Apples

If you have never tried a slice of apple pie with a slice of cheese, get ready to enjoy an easy version that is quite tasty and surprising. This sweet pie gets a new twist with the richness of cheese, without the trouble of making a pie from scratch. A favorite memory of my mother was eating a slice of apple pie covered in melted cheese when she was expecting her first child.

Preheat oven to 350 degrees

2 14 oz. cans sliced unsweetened apples
1 8 oz. jar of Cheese Whiz®
1 c. sugar
1 c. plain flour

Grease a 9 X 13 casserole dish with cooking spray. Place the apples and liquid uniformly in the bottom of the dish. (Do not drain) In a small mixing bowl, combine Cheese Whiz®, sugar and flour until well blended. Spoon the mixture over the apples evenly. Bake in preheated oven for 25 to 30 minutes, or until lightly brown.

Creamy Mashed Potatoes

2 lbs. Idaho potatoes
1 qt. water
½ stick margarine
1 ½ c. sour cream
Salt and Pepper to taste

Peel and rinse potatoes in cold water. Cut potatoes into 2 inch cubes. Place potatoes and water in a medium size stock pot. Bring to a boil on high heat. Reduce heat to medium low and cover. Cook 15 to 20 minutes or until potatoes are fork tender. Remove from heat and drain water. Add margarine, salt and pepper. With a hand mixer, beat until smooth. Add sour cream and continue beating until smooth and creamy. Return to low heat, cover until ready to serve.

Yeast Muffin Surprise

4 c. self-rising flour
1/4 c. sugar
1/2 c. very warm water
1 envelope active dry yeast
1 ½ c. milk
2 sticks of margarine

In a medium size microwavable bowl, melt margarine on high for 1 minute. Remove from microwave. In a small mixing bowl, mix yeast with warm water until dissolved. Stir with a wire whisk into the melted margarine until evenly distributed. Add the milk and stir until well blended. Blend in flour and sugar, stirring to form a soft dough that resembles a very thick batter. Dough will appear somewhat lumpy. Drop by heaping tablespoons into greased muffin tin until half full. Bake on 400 degrees for 15 to 20 minutes until golden brown. Yields 24 muffins.

*I frequently cut this recipe in half to serve for evening meals. You may make the entire recipe and store the remaining dough in the refrigerator for 2 to 3 days.

Stews, Soups, One Dish Meals and Trimmings

Chicken Stew

Vegetable Soup

Chicken Mull

Buster's Chicken and Vegetables

Beef Stew

Waldorf Salad

Fried Corn Bread

Chicken Stew

3 to 4 lb. fryer
2 to 3 qts. water
2 ribs celery hearts, sliced thin
1 large carrot, julienned
1 tsp. black pepper
1 tsp. salt
2 c. half and half
½ stick margarine

Thickener
½ c. plain flour
1 c. water
Stir together with a whisk until smooth.

Wash chicken and place in a 4 qt. stock pot with enough water to just cover the bird. Add salt and pepper. Bring to a boil. Reduce heat to simmer and cover. Simmer for 1 to ½ hours, until the breast is fork tender. Remove bird from stock pot and debone, tearing the meat into bite size pieces. Place the chicken back into the chicken broth, add vegetables. Return to a boil on high heat. Reduce heat and cook 20 minutes to tender the vegetables. While cooking, make thickener and set aside. Add butter to chicken and vegetables, and then slowly add half and half, increasing the heat to medium high. When the stew starts to bubble, remove from heat. Slowly add the thickener to desired consistency. Continue stirring until smooth. Spoon into bowls and serve with saltines. Cornbread is also delicious with the stew.

*If you prefer white meat, add 4 breasts to the stock pot with the chicken. Debone the chicken, discarding the dark meat. The fryer provides a rich stock for the stew, unlike boneless breasts. Bone-in breasts with the skin on may be used, if desired.

Vegetable Soup

The original preparation of this soup started with 4 oz. of lean salt pork added to the first quart of water. This newer and healthier version of this recipe proves to be just as tasty. You may add the salt pork if desired. Fresh vegetables are always best if in season, but if not the frozen ones work as well.

10 oz. bag frozen or 2 c. fresh tiny baby lima beans
1 medium onion, thinly sliced into 1 inch pieces
1 bell pepper, coarsely chopped
2 c. cabbage, cut into 1 inch pieces
10 oz. frozen bag or 3 c. fresh okra, sliced
10 oz. frozen bag or 2 c. fresh cut corn
3 large cans of whole tomatoes, hand chopped *or*
12 medium size fresh tomatoes peeled and chopped (I prefer to use the more rich flavor of canned tomatoes)
2 qts. of water

In a large stock pot, bring 1 quart of water to a boil on high heat. Add the butterbeans, and bring back to a boil. Reduce heat to low and cover. Cook for 30 minutes. Add onion, pepper and cabbage and the remaining quart of water. Bring back to a boil on high heat, reduce heat to low, cover and simmer for 30 more minutes. Add corn, okra, carrots, and tomatoes. Again, bring back to a boil on high heat, stirring to distribute vegetables. Cover and reduce heat and cook for an additional 30 minutes on simmer. Distinguish heat and allow soup to rest for 30 minutes to an hour for flavors to marry. Soup will be more flavorful as the flavors blend and is even better the next day. Yields 4 quarts and freezes beautifully

.
Potatoes can be added during the last 30 minutes, but do not freeze well. You may cook cubed fresh potatoes separately and add during the heating process, when soup has been removed from the freezer.

*Green beans may be substituted for butterbeans or as an addition.

Chicken Mull

This version of stewing chicken achieves a similar result as a chicken stew. The recipe is a favorite of our family. It originated from a men's club in Middle Georgia that met periodically. Interestingly enough, it was served with fried chicken. My version has all white meat. To get the best stock, I actually cook two whole chickens, de-bone and use only the white meat, along with 6 to 8 bone-in chicken breasts. That of course is a personal preference.

2 whole chickens
Salt and black pepper to taste

In a large stock pot, cook chicken in 2 quarts of water. Bring to a boil, cover, reduce heat and simmer for 1 hour. Remove chicken from pot and debone. Add the chicken back to the water and return to a boil. Reduce heat again to simmer and cook another one to two hours, stirring often, until chicken is stringy and fine. Add salt and black pepper to taste. To achieve the best results, liberally use the black pepper.

Serve over toast points. Sweet pickle midgets or slices are an excellent accompaniment.

Buster's Chicken and Vegetables

4-6 Chicken Breasts, bone-in
1 large sweet onion, peeled, halved and then quartered
20-24 baby carrots, washed and peeled
12-16 small red potatoes, washed and halved
1 10 ½ oz. can chicken broth
1 can of French style green beans, drained (2 cans if serving 6)
1¼ c. water
1 tsp. black pepper
1 tsp. salt
2 tbl. butter
2 tbl. vegetable oil
3 sprigs fresh or ½ tsp. dried rosemary

In a Dutch oven, melt butter on medium heat, add oil. Place chicken in oven and brown, then remove from pot. Add the onions, potatoes and carrots to pan drippings. Sauté, stirring gently for about five minutes to disperse the vegetables and distribute drippings. Remove vegetables and set aside. Add the chicken broth and water to the drippings, to raise the sediment, gently scraping the bottom of the oven. Return the chicken and vegetables to the oven. Sprinkle with salt and black pepper. Place rosemary on top of chicken and vegetables. Cook for 1 hour on the stovetop. Baste the chicken and vegetables often. 15 minutes prior to completion of baking, pour the drained green beans in one section of the Dutch oven. When cooking time has been completed, remove from oven. Using a slotted spoon, arrange chicken and vegetables on a serving platter.

*You may cook in a large oven proof casserole by placing the chicken and vegetables in the dish. Pour the liquid from the Dutch oven over the chicken and vegetables, adding the seasonings as instructed above. When adding the green beans, pour half of the beans each on opposite sides of the casserole dish, for an attractive offering to serve on a buffet. You may serve with a salad and bread, if desired.

Beef Stew

3 to 4 lbs. of lean stew beef
2 tbl. cooking oil
2 quarts of water
2 medium onions, quartered and then sliced thin
4 large sized peeled potatoes, quartered and cubed
3 ribs celery hearts, cut into 2" pieces
2 to 3 c. baby carrots, peeled
1 large can of *V-8 Juice*®
1 tsp. salt
1 tsp. black pepper

In a Dutch oven over medium high heat, brown beef in oil. Add onions and spices stirring well. Reduce heat and simmer 1 hour or until beef is fork tender, stirring occasionally. Add the V-8 Juice®, water and vegetables. Bring to a boil over medium high heat. Reduce heat to a simmer and cook 30 more minutes, or until vegetables are fork tender. Serve with cornbread muffins that have been sweetened.

Waldorf Salad

2 c. diced red apples, skin on
2 c. diced Granny Smith apples, skin on
16 oz. can of mandarin oranges, drained and cut in half
2/3 c. chopped walnuts or nuts of your choice
¼ c. mayonnaise

Place ingredients in a medium mixing bowl. Gently stir together and serve in your favorite glass bowl. This salad is festive and a great compliment to pork, especially when other fruits are out of season. It is also a nice side dish for stews.

Fried Corn Bread

I had never heard of hard cornbread until I was introduced to it by MaMa. The key to making it is to have good cornmeal. You must use plain meal that is finely ground. The version below is mine, maybe not as good, but my family likes it. I rarely cook it, due to the grease content, but here goes - a recipe worth trying once.

Pre-heat oven to 400 degrees.

1 c. finely ground cornmeal, plain
Enough water to make it the slightly thicker than pancake batter and less thick than cornbread batter.
Corn oil or vegetable oil. Canola would be fine, but I would not suggest olive oil.
Salt to taste

Prepare batter using cornmeal and water. Use a shallow iron skillet, if you have one, if not a thick baking pan. Pour a little less than ½ inch of oil into the skillet. Place in the oven until the oil is hot, about 5 to 7 minutes. Remove from oven and spoon ¼ cups of batter into the hot oil. Continue until the pan is covered. The batter will form into round to oblong as it touches the oil, making each piece of the bread easy to separate when cooked. Work quickly as the oil will cool and the batter must be returned to the oven as soon possible. Bake about 20 minutes on 400 degrees until the bread is lightly brown on top and a darker, more golden brown on the bottom. When you remove from oven, again work quickly to remove the bread and drain on paper toweling. The cakes of bread will be somewhat gooey in the middle. Sprinkle with salt. Serve with butter or margarine, if desired. The cakes are delicious with turnip greens, peas or butterbeans.

Relish Sinfully Southern Selections

Fish Slaw

Hushpuppies

Frances' Salt Pork and Gravy

Dororie's Salt Pork and Gravy

Dove Pie

MaMa's Barbeque Sauce

Fish Slaw

Not only did my daddy fish, he took us fishing also. It was not uncommon for him to come home with a catch of fifty to one hundred fish. He allowed us to help him "dress the fish," as he called it. We learned to scale the fish, under his ever watchful eye. They were stinky and smelly, but we all wanted to be a part of the undertaking. My mother would freeze them and soon we would have a wonderful fish fry. Her famous cole slaw follows:

1 large cabbage
1 bell pepper
1 large fresh tomato
Mayonnaise – use sparingly until quantity desired
Dill pickle relish, drained and added to taste
Pepper to taste

Wash the cabbage and slice in wedges from top to bottom on all four sides, then across the bottom, removing the core. Using a cutting board, place each wedge, cut side down and slice lengthwise in thin slices, creating an angel hair effect in the slices. Continue with each wedge until all cabbage had been sliced. Place in a large serving bowl with a lid for easy storage. Using a hand chopper, chop the slices until they are the consistency desired. If an electric chopper is used, it will create a watery slaw and the cabbage may need to be drained with a colander. Add the dill pickle relish, pepper and mayonnaise to taste. Slice bell pepper in rings, or slices to use as a garnishment and for added flavor. Cube tomatoes and top the slaw. You may sprinkle some fresh ground pepper, if desired. Do not add salt, as the dill pickle relish will season.

Hushpuppies

Hushpuppies were prepared often in our household, because fish was so abundant. In my estimation, you cannot serve fish without hushpuppies. These crispy pieces of heaven have been sorely missed as the supply of my Daddy's fresh fish dwindled over the years, even long before his death. The days of the "fish fry" have long since become a memory, one that will never be forgotten.

1 ¾ c. white corn meal
1 egg, well beaten
1 c. buttermilk
1 small onion, diced
4 c. peanut oil

Combine the above ingredients in a medium size mixing bowl until smooth and thick. Set aside for 10 to 15 minutes. The meal will rise and become thicker.

In an electric fryer or heavy skillet, heat peanut oil on medium high until it sizzles when a sprinkle of corn meal is dropped into it. Stir the hushpuppy batter well and then fill a heaping ice cream scoop with the batter, releasing into the hot oil by scoops, until there is a layer of hushpuppies. Immediately turn the hushpuppies individually as the edges appear brown. Turn over again individually until they are lightly browned on all sides. Remove with a slotted spoon, shaking excess oil as the hushpuppy is being removed. Place on paper toweling. Immediately transfer to a brown paper bag to keep temperature to an optimum until ready to serve.

*Finely diced jalapenos, bell pepper or pimentos may be added to the batter. ½ c. cream style corn may be substituted for ½ c. of the buttermilk to create a creamy texture inside the hushpuppy.

Frances Salt Pork and Gravy

8 slices of pre-sliced salt pork
1 c. self- rising flour, sifted
2 c. water
½ tsp. pepper
2 c. vegetable oil

Rinse excess salt from pre-sliced meat. In a medium size mixing bowl combine flour, water and pepper. Using a wire whisk, stir until smooth. Add the meat slices to the batter. In a medium size iron skillet, heat 1 cup of vegetable oil on medium high heat until the oil sizzles when a pinch of flour is added. Remove meat slices from the batter individually, allowing excess batter to drain into mixing bowl, then add meat to hot grease. You may adjust heat as the meat will start to brown quickly. Brown meat lightly on both sides. Remove from the skillet and allow oil to drain on paper toweling.

Gravy:
2 heaping tbl. self-rising flour
1 ½ to 2 c. water
½ tsp. salt
½ tsp. pepper

Stir flour into salt pork drippings and continue stirring to make a dark brown roué. Reduce heat to low. Immediately add the water, stirring constantly. The gravy will become thick and may require additional water to achieve the consistency you desire. Add salt and pepper. Serve over open face biscuits with meat on the side. Add additional pepper if desired.

*Steamed cabbage is a wonderful accompaniment to the side meat.

Dorrie's Salt Pork and Gravy

Streak o' lean (a.k.a. salt pork) and gravy has always been considered a delicacy in our family. The dish has been coveted by the Aunts who never seemed to master the art of preparation. The requests by the men and women alike in my family when visiting my grandmother were always the same, "Streak O' lean and gravy for breakfast, please, and don't forget the biscuits!"

8 slices of pre-sliced salt pork
2 heaping tbl. self-rising flour
1 ½ to 2 c. milk
½ tsp. salt
½ tsp. pepper

Rinse excess salt from pre-sliced meat. Place meat slices in an iron skillet, and cook over medium high heat until brown and crispy. Remove to paper toweling to drain. Stir flour into drippings and continue stirring to make a dark brown roué. Add the milk slowly, stirring constantly. The gravy will become thick and may require additional milk to achieve the consistency you desire. Add salt and pepper to taste. Serve over open face biscuits with meat on the side. (The meat is very salty and is mostly "nibbled" if consumed – personal preference)

*Add additional pepper if desired, but most highly recommended!
*Serve with fresh sliced tomatoes when in season

MaMa's Barbeque Sauce

MaMa and DeDaddy owned a country store at one time. They prepared and sold barbequed pork. Their specialty was pork sandwiches. Of course, cooking the pork is an art in itself. Try this wonderful sauce on your hickory smoked pork, or if you are not so inclined, purchase pork that has not been "sauced".

1 quart white vinegar
46 oz. tomato juice
8 oz. lemon juice
18 oz. Kraft Original Barbeque Sauce®
½ c. Worcestershire sauce
¼ c. oil
Salt to taste
2 tbl. black pepper
½ tsp. hot sauce
1/3 c. sugar
1 tsp. red pepper

Mix and cook in a large stock pot, until it cooks down to a depth of about 2 inches.

Dove Pie

Pre-heat oven to 350 degrees

10 to 12 fresh breast of dove
Water to cover
1 tsp. salt
1 tsp. pepper
2 c. milk
½ c. of self-rising flour
1 c. of water
1/ 2 stick of melted margarine

In a large stock pot, add salt, pepper and just enough water to cover the dove. Bring to a boil on high heat, cover and reduce heat to low. Cook for 45 minutes, to one hour, or until the birds are fork tender. Remove birds from broth and place in a greased 9 X 13 casserole dish or baking pan. Whisk together self-rising flour and the remaining cup of water, until smooth and creamy. Bring broth back to a boil on medium high heat. Slowly add the flour mixture to the broth, stirring constantly, until it becomes thickened. Next, add the milk into the broth, continuing to stir until the broth becomes bubbly. Pour the mixture over the dove in the prepared pan, so that the birds are only half submerged. Excess broth may be discarded. Place prepared crust over the dove. Bake at 350 degrees until crust is golden brown. Remove from oven and brush with melted margarine.

Crust:
1 stick of margarine, cold
2 c. self- rising flour
1c. whole buttermilk

Place the flour in a medium sized mixing bowl. Cut the margarine in with a pastry cutter or use gloved hand, until the margarine has been distributed throughout and pieces are the size of a dime. Add the buttermilk and gently blend with spoon or hand, until all flour has been incorporated and forms a soft dough. Place the dough on a well- floured pastry sheet. Sprinkle the dough with excess flour and knead the dough to the center from the edges, incorporating enough flour to allow it to be rolled out into a sheet, without sticking to a rolling pin. Using a floured rolling pin, roll the dough into a rectangular shape that is ¼ inch in thickness and large enough to cover the 9 X 13 inch pan.

Epilogue

And so there it is, the humble story of my life as I have lived thus far, measured not in fame or fortune, but in moments of love and compassion, culminating into the realization that cooking is my gift to share with those I love. If there is one thing for certain, we are all the product of our surroundings – family, friends and the mysteries of God's beauty that is freely given by just opening our eyes. Relish your family and friends, but most of all, relish your memories, for they are the footprints of the mind and define us all!

Index of Recipes

Made in the USA
Lexington, KY
15 November 2019